CO-ATN-929

JEFF
GORDON

NASCAR Driver

Michael Benson

Ferguson
An imprint of ☑®Facts On File

Jeff Gordon: NASCAR Driver

Ferguson
An imprint of Facts On File, Inc.
132 West 31st Street
New York NY 10001

Library of Congress Cataloging-in-Publication Data

Benson, Michael.
  Jeff Gordon : NASCAR driver / Michael Benson.
    p. cm.
  Includes bibliographical references and index.
  ISBN 0-8160-5885-7 (hc : alk. paper)
  1. Gordon, Jeff, 1971– 2. Stock car drivers—United States—Biography. I. Title.
  GV1032.G67B46 2005
  796.72′092—dc22
                                                                2004011347

Ferguson books are available at special discounts when purchased in bulk quantities for businesses, associations, institutions, or sales promotions. Please call our Special Sales Department in New York at (212) 967-8800 or (800) 322-8755.

You can find Ferguson on the World Wide Web at http://www.fergpubco.com

Text design by David Strelecky

Pages 109–120 adapted from Ferguson's *Encyclopedia of Careers and Vocational Guidance, Twelfth Edition*

Printed in the United States of America

MP Hermitage 10 9 8 7 6 5 4 3 2 1

This book is printed on acid-free paper.

CONTENTS

1

SIX HUNDRED WINS BY AGE 18

The most popular spectator sport in the United States is not baseball. It's not football or basketball either. America's most popular sport is automobile racing.

To the outsider, it looks simple. You get in your car and keep the accelerator pressed down as far as your foot can push it. As you hurtle around the track, you expect your crew to keep your car in perfect condition, and you try not to go deaf as you weave your machine through traffic toward the checkered flag.

Of course, it's not anywhere near that easy. Just as football is not a simple matter of "catch the ball and try not to get tackled," so, too, racing involves skills that might not be immediately visible to the eye.

So what does it take to be a world-class race car driver? The more you know about the lives of the greats, the more it becomes clear that each successful driver is also an extraordinary person in many ways.

Each is an athlete, gifted with unusual vision, coordination—and the will to win. The concentration necessary to operate a car at faster than 200 miles per hour over the course of a long afternoon, when a momentary lapse can result in serious injuries or death, is phenomenal.

In addition, the top drivers are good businessmen. They know how to put together a winning team. They find sponsors to put them in competitive cars. They trust their crew to make sure that their car always is in peak performance condition. With every race day they must consider a host of factors: weather, the other racers, track condition, and how the car is handling that day. Without everything working just right, a driver does not have a chance of winning.

Drivers are strong, self-confident, resilient, and willing to take risks. In fact, they *have* to be all those things in order to win.

Jeff Gordon is just such a driver—and he is a winner.

With the help of a supportive mom and dad, Jeff is a former "kid phenom." Before Jeff turned 18 years old, he had already won more than 600 races behind the wheel of a car.

Jeff Gordon is one of the greatest drivers in the history of stock car racing. (Landov)

One quality that does not matter in racing is size. Jeff is not a big guy. At 5-foot-7, 150 pounds, he might have been too small to play football or basketball, but in auto racing his size was an advantage. It was that much easier for him to squeeze in and out of his race cars.

As an adult Jeff has quickly become one of the greatest NASCAR drivers in stock car racing history—and this is his story.

2

"KNOW WHAT YOU WANT TO ACHIEVE"

Jeff Gordon was born August 4, 1971, in Vallejo, California. About a month later, Jeff's mom and dad separated. Jeff's mother, Carol, decided to raise Jeff and his sister Kim on her own. Kim was four when Jeff was born.

While Kim was easy to raise, Jeff turned out to be a handful. He was constantly on the move, getting into this and that, and he was stubborn. If he wanted to do something he was determined to do it, regardless of what his mother said.

Most kids ride a tricycle when they are little and then move up to a bicycle with training wheels. After some practice, the training wheels come off. Jeff did not bother with the first two stages. He got on a two-wheeler with no training wheels when he was three years old, and had no problem riding it the first time he tried.

Carol worked at a medical-supply company. While working there, she met a man named John Bickford. John built products that helped people with disabilities drive cars. In his spare time, he built parts for race cars. John and Carol liked each other and began dating. Before long John and Carol were married and John became Jeff and Kim's stepfather.

"As far as I was concerned, John was my father from the get-go," Jeff later said.

It was John who adapted the smallest two-wheel bicycle available so that Jeff could ride it even though he was only three. Jeff rode his bike alongside older kids in the neighborhood on a bike course a few blocks from his house. After a year, when Jeff was four, he began to race his bike in organized bike-racing leagues for kids. John was his crew chief (the leader of Jeff's racing team).

Jeff's first races were on his BMX bicycle dashing around the block ahead of the neighbor kids. Jeff was only about half the size of the other kids in the races. At age four he was racing against eight- and nine-year-olds.

Among the important lessons that John taught Jeff early on was the importance of setting goals.

"Know what you want to achieve," John would say, "then focus all of your energy on it."

Bike racing was dangerous. Kids were getting hurt all the time. Jeff often ended up at the bottom of a huge pile of racers after crashes, but was never seriously injured. Some other kid might have broken a bone and needed a ride to the hospital, but luckily Jeff's worst injuries were scrapes and bruises. He always seemed to pop out of the pile with a smile on his face.

It was clear that Jeff was never happier than when he was going really fast. His parents could tell how much he loved speed. Carol was worried that it was only a matter of time before Jeff was hurt more seriously on his bike, so John suggested he switch to racing small cars.

First Car

Jeff's stepfather worked in auto parts and knew race cars. He could tell that Jeff had the talent to be a race car driver when he grew up, so before he could even read, Jeff was behind the wheel of a car.

Jeff's first car was what is called a *quarter midget,* an undersized car suitable to be raced by a child. John came home one day with two quarter-midget race cars. One was painted black and the other pink. Jeff quickly claimed the black one and the pink one was used for spare parts.

With wheels the size of those found on a lawn mower, and roll bars to protect the driver if the car flipped over, the cars could go about 25 miles per hour. John convinced Carol that quarter-midget races were actually safer than bike races.

"A bike has two wheels," John told Jeff's mother, "and this has four. He is strapped into the car. There is a roll cage around him. He'll be wearing a full-face helmet."

So Jeff drove his first race car at the age of four and a half. However, before John would let Jeff race in his new car, Jeff had to prove to his stepfather that he could drive like an expert.

To practice, they went to the nearby Solano County Fairgrounds where they fashioned a fifth of a mile track out of a seldom-used parking lot. Jeff ran thousands of laps on that track, until he knew his new car inside out. Jeff quickly learned to love driving, and it was just as quickly clear that he was very good at it.

Bickford later said, "We'd take that car out every night after I got home from work and run it lap after lap. Jeff couldn't seem to get enough of it."

The little cars that Jeff drove were not designed to go very fast, and they were tough, difficult to harm. But Bickford could see into the future, into a world in which running into things could not only cause expensive damage but could also cause severe physical injuries.

No Bumping

In order to prepare Jeff for a future in racing, John made a rule that if Jeff was in a race and he bumped into another car or into the barriers that marked the sides of the track (usually rubber tires), he would not be allowed to accept a trophy—even if he won the race. Thus, while other kids might have treated their midget racers like bumper cars, Jeff learned before he started kindergarten that driving your car into something could be very bad.

The other lesson John taught Jeff early on was the need for complete concentration. He told Jeff that when he was driving a race car, he could not have anything else on his mind.

Bickford later said, "Jeff had superb hand-eye coordination, learned rapidly, and developed a rhythm. We worked on all that."

Jeff's eyesight was better than normal as well. No matter how fast he was moving on a racetrack, he could see things that were far up ahead, as well as things that were close by. He understood where he was on the track, as well as where all of the other cars were. If something happened up ahead that made it necessary for him to slow down, he would react to it a fraction of a second faster than other drivers.

Jeff's even temper and good-natured personality also made him a natural racer. When a driver is behind the wheel of a car, 100 percent concentration is a must. If another driver cuts that person off or prevents him from passing, the driver cannot get angry. That moment of anger could cause the slight mistake that might result in an accident. And accidents at fast speeds hurt not only the drivers who cause them, but also the innocent drivers who might be in the wrong place at the wrong time.

Sleeping in the Back of the Pickup

Jeff began to race in organized quarter-midget races all over California. There was a race going on somewhere just about every weekend, and John and Jeff would always go, often sleeping in the back of the family pickup truck.

Jeff did not do that well during his first year of car racing, however. Even after he reached his fifth birthday, he was still by far the youngest driver out there and the age difference showed. Jeff wanted to go faster than was physically possible. He would go too fast into the curves and tended to spin out a lot.

One problem Jeff had was how to pass cars and how to get through traffic made up of slower cars. He could run lap after lap practicing by himself, but he could only practice passing skills when in an actual race.

Then Jeff came up with an idea. He asked John to buy Carol her own midget car. That way Jeff and his mom could practice together. She could run in front of him and he could practice passing her.

By the time he was six years old, Jeff knew how fast to go into the curves, and he stopped spinning out. He began to win races—and he has not stopped winning since.

John continued to bring home new cars, until the family had eight or nine of them parked out in the yard. John had been one of 10 children and often had not received any of the things he wanted when he was younger. Now, through Jeff, he was having a second childhood—and he made no effort to hide it.

Whereas the kids Jeff was racing against would race in maybe 20 races a year and usually just those during summer vacation, Jeff raced every week all year. By the time Jeff was in first grade, car racing had become his life.

His age became an advantage rather than a disadvantage. Because all of the cars were basically the same and Jeff was smaller than the other drivers, his car had to carry less weight, a difference that showed up in Jeff's superior speed.

John later said, "All of the other parents were saying that Jeff was probably lying about his age, that he was probably 20, and just really little."

By 1978, at age seven, Jeff was dominating quarter-midget racing. During the entire year Jeff never qualified for a race with anything other than the fastest time. He won 35 races that year, many more than most kids even entered.

Grand National Champion

In 1979 things got even better. Jeff raced on the national quarter-midget circuit. He won 52 main events—an average of one per week for the entire year. Jeff won his local quarter-midget racing championship and got to race in the Grand National Championship in Denver, Colorado. He won that, too. So future NASCAR champ Jeff Gordon won his first national racing championship at the age of eight.

Jeff's domination began hurting the sport. Kids who normally would have raced decided against it because, with Jeff in the race, they had no chance of winning. For the first time many tracks began to offer second- and third-place trophies to hold contestants' interest.

By the time Jeff was nine he was competing against, and regularly beating, teenagers. To make sure that Jeff missed as little school as possible, he would often fly back home from national competitions alone, while John drove.

Graduating to Go-Karts

In 1981, after five years of driving quarter-midgets cars, 10-year-old Jeff graduated to go-karts, another type of race car suitable for a child, but larger than the quarter midgets and three times as powerful. The go-kart tracks, like the cars themselves, were much larger than the tracks Jeff had previously conquered. The same was true of the drivers. Many of the racers Jeff was now competing against were finishing high school. He had just turned 10. There was no age rule because, as Jeff put it, "Nobody was fool enough to drive that young."

The older kids did not like the idea of a little kid trying to compete with them, so Jeff was not treated very nicely

Go-kart racing (Landov)

on or around the go-kart tracks. "The other drivers were tough," Jeff later said.

But the rough treatment did absolutely nothing to discourage Jeff—or slow him down—in the least. In his first year of go-karting he raced in 25 events and won all of them.

By the mid-1980s Jeff's racing not only dominated his life, it was dominating his family's life. Then a new problem cropped up: boredom. Jeff raced in about 150 races during 1982 and 1983 and won so easily and so often that the thrill was gone.

To mix things up a little bit and keep life interesting for Jeff, John and Carol sent him to water-skiing school. As might be expected, he was far and away the best water skier the school had ever seen. After two weeks of lessons his teacher told John that Jeff was good enough to water-ski professionally.

But Jeff wanted to be the best water skier in the world. When he looked at the champions of the sport, he noticed they were all tall and lanky. Jeff had short legs and arms. He continued water skiing for fun, but it did not become an obsession. Racing was still his thing.

John and Carol understood the importance of keeping Jeff busy. Without something constructive to do, Jeff tended to hang around with the wrong crowd and, as he put it, "get into mischief."

Sprint Cars

John decided that Jeff was ready to take the next step: He would race in a sprint car, a type of race car that could go as fast as 135 mph. Sprint cars are full-size automobiles with engines up to 70 times more powerful than those found in go-karts. They could go from zero to 60 miles per hour in under three seconds. With their open tops and roll cages, however, sprint cars do look a bit like oversize go-karts.

A friend of John's built a sprint car for Jeff, and they took the car and Jeff out to a country road to practice. Jeff admits that he was a little nervous when he first got behind the wheel of the sprint car—but he quickly learned to handle it.

Skill was not the problem. Jeff had what it took. Now age was a problem. Because the sprint car was a full-fledged automobile, racers had to be 16 years old and have a driver's license to drive one in California.

Jeff was three years away from having a driver's license. So, John searched for a sprint car circuit that did not have an age requirement. During February of 1985, he learned of the All-Star sprint car series in Florida. Soon thereafter John and Jeff were crossing the country, heading for Jacksonville, Florida, for Jeff's first sprint car race.

That first race did not go well. Around the track it was obvious that most people did not approve of a 13-year-old entering the race.

"People were looking at us like we were crazy when they found out I was the driver," Jeff said.

When Jeff tried to enter the competition, the head track official said, "No way."

John did some fast-talking about Jeff's skill and his experience. He also pointed out that there was no rule preventing Jeff from being on the track. The official eventually gave in, but made John sign a waiver—a contract that said he would not sue the track if Jeff were injured. He also said that Jeff had to start from the back of the pack. When race time came, Jeff was in his car and ready to go.

Lined up for the start of the race, preparing to race against adults for the first time in his life, Jeff's nerves got the best of him. He hit the accelerator and immediately spun out.

"I did my best to hold the line," Jeff later said, "but the back end got a little loose and my right rear tire scraped the wall."

The car was undamaged but Jeff's ego was severely dented. A few minutes later rain began to fall hard and the night's racing was quickly canceled. Any other kid might have given up at that point, but Jeff chalked it up to experience and was determined to do better the next time.

John and Jeff hitched up the sprint car and hit the road. They traveled across Florida to East Bay Raceway in

Tampa where the next sprint car race was scheduled. In Tampa, Jeff did much better. He didn't finish near the front, but he didn't crash either.

Going to the Pay Window

The best thing about that weekend in Florida, Jeff remembers, is that he got paid for racing for the first time. Finishing 18th out of 54, he went to the pay window where he was handed $300 in cash.

From then on, things continued to improve. Two weeks later, Jeff finished in second place. The national press began to notice the boy wonder. ESPN ran a story about Jeff on its *Speedweek* show.

When summer vacation started, John and Jeff traveled around the Midwest, where there also was no age limit for sprint car drivers. Jeff raced in 22 events in all and finished in second place twice, at the KC Raceway in Chillicothe, Ohio, and at Bloomington Speedway in Bloomington, Indiana.

After a year of sprint races, Jeff experienced what he would later call "one of the highlights of my career." It was 1986 and Jeff was now 14. The race was in Tampa, at the same track where he ran his first sprint car race—not counting the disaster at Jacksonville, of course. Jeff got to race against one of his heroes, Steve Kinser, who was considered the king of sprint cars.

Jeff ran in front of Kinser for much of the race. Although Kinser eventually passed Jeff, he managed to hold the legend back lap after lap. When the race was over, Kinser took time to tell Jeff what a great race he had run.

"Kid, you're going to be a good one," Kinser said. It was a compliment Jeff never forgot.

Good-bye, California

The trips back to California were starting to become grueling. The family had to make a choice: wait three years for Jeff to get his California driver's license, or move to the Midwest where the races were.

The choice was easy: The family said good-bye to California.

"I loved our town and my friends," Jeff later said, "but at the time California was no place for a teenage race car driver. I couldn't even race in my own state. So my mom and dad decided we would move to Indiana, where open-wheel racing is the state sport."

In 1986 the Bickfords moved to the small town of Pittsboro, Indiana, not far from Indianapolis.

Jeff appreciated the sacrifices his mother and stepfather made for him. "I owe my whole career to John and my mom," Jeff later said. "I wouldn't be a race car driver if not for John, and mom made a lot of sacrifices, too. My parents were my role models and set a lot of examples."

Jeff was seen as a regular guy at Tri-West High School in Pittsboro. He was popular and folks from the town remember him fondly. But he was not a normal teenager. He admits that he never really had a best friend. Racing was his life. There was no time for anything else. Even on his graduation night, when the other kids were going from party to party, Jeff had to go to the racetrack, where he was competing in a sprint car race.

Twice in 1986, Jeff got to travel abroad and race. He drove for a New Zealand car owner named John Rae. The first trip was to Australia. Jeff loved the country but did not run well in the races. Later in the year he traveled to New Zealand.

Jeff remembers being picked up at the airport in a limousine and being put up in a suite at a fancy hotel, both luxuries that he had never experienced before. This trip was much more successful on the track. Jeff ran in 15 races in New Zealand and won 14 of them.

Although Jeff continued to win a lot of races, he was not getting rich at it. These were not NASCAR events or the Indianapolis 500 he was winning. These were local tracks and Jeff was racing against weekend drivers—men and women who had regular jobs but raced, mostly for fun, on the weekends. Jeff was barely making enough money to keep his race cars in parts. Luckily, John was pretty handy. In some cases John could make auto parts for Jeff's race cars instead of buying them.

Because high school was a lot tougher than grammar school, Jeff did not travel as much as he had when he was younger. Instead, he usually raced at the same track every weekend, the nearby Bloomington Speedway.

Some of Jeff's teachers went out of their way to make Jeff's racing and schooling one and the same. His science teacher, for example, always allowed Jeff to do his reports on racing engines and aerodynamics.

The Major League of Sprint Car Racing

In 1988 Jeff raced in dirt-track races sanctioned by USAC (United States Automobile Club), which is the major league of sprint car racing. He won his first USAC race in Florence, Kentucky.

So that he could race more than once a week, he also took up midget car racing, another form of racing sanctioned by USAC. In many cases, Jeff would be able to race in his sprint car and in his midget car during the same day (or night) at the same racetrack. The midget races did not pay as much money as the sprint cars, but Jeff loved driving them.

Jeff drove for several car owners during his teen years, and in a variety of cars. But one thing always stayed the same. John was always there, enjoying the thrills, while making sure that no one took advantage of his kid.

The first "big race" Jeff ever ran in was the 500-Mile Race held at Indianapolis Raceway Park in late May. This is not to be confused with the Indianapolis (or "Indy") 500 run at the Indianapolis Motor Speedway the next day. Jeff's race was the warm-up event for the "Greatest Spectacle in Racing" and was held at the smaller track at Raceway Park. But it was still by far the biggest (and longest) race Jeff had ever raced in. It was big enough to be shown live on ESPN. Still a few weeks shy of graduating from high school, Jeff won the race and impressed everyone with his post-race interview. Jeff made sure that he thanked his sponsors and his car owner before he said anything about himself.

The racing world had been given official notice. This was a kid who was going places—in a hurry.

3

CHOOSING STOCK CARS

When Jeff graduated from high school in 1989, he was, for the first time, able to dedicate all of his time to racing. He now had to decide on the type of racing he wanted to do.

There was the Formula One Grand Prix circuit, which would have taken him to races in exotic places all around the world. The only way to race Formula One, Jeff decided, was to live in Europe, and he did not feel he was ready for that.

There were the Indy car leagues—the cars that ran in the Indy 500—in the United States. But there were more drivers than there were cars, so it would be difficult for Jeff to break into those leagues, as well.

During the summer of 1990, while still only 18 years old, Jeff took a big step toward moving up to the major leagues of car racing when he attended Buck Baker's driving school in Rockingham, North Carolina. Buck was a

Unlike other types of race cars, NASCAR stock cars are meant to resemble cars anyone might own. (Landov)

NASCAR legend, and the father of fellow NASCAR super-star Buddy Baker.

Here is how it came about: John had made friends with an ESPN racing announcer named Larry Nuber who had talked to Buck about Jeff. The two formulated a deal: If Jeff attended the driving school, ESPN would send a crew to the school and do a feature on the "phenom new kid." The deal was good for Jeff, good for the school, and good for ESPN.

NASCAR race cars do not look like race cars. They are built so that they look like a car your family might own. Jeff only had to drive a top-notch stock car for a couple of laps on the North Carolina Motor Speedway before he decided that this was what he wanted to do. He loved the feel of the car, and he loved the high banking in the corners that allowed him to make turns without slowing down.

Years after his first ride in a stock car, Jeff told a reporter: "That first day, the first time I got into a stock car, I said, 'This is it. This is what I want to do.' The car was different from anything that I was used to. It was so big and heavy. It felt very fast but very smooth. I loved it."

Birth of Stock Car Racing

Stock car racing, which would come to define Jeff's career, has quite a colorful history. Stock car driving was invented in the 1930s. Drivers who hauled moonshine (illegal liquor) used to gather in Georgia and race against one another on a track that had been cut out of a cow pasture.

Driving fast was nothing new for these men. They drove fast as part of their job because they had to outrun the law enforcement agents who were chasing them. The story goes that the purse for the first stock car race was a case of corn liquor.

Bill France Sr., who owned a gas station in Florida, figured there was money to be made selling tickets to see the drivers race around the track, and in 1948 NASCAR—

the National Association of Stock Car Automobile Racing—was born.

Some of the most popular stock car races take place in Daytona and Indianapolis. The first Daytona races were not held on a real track at all, but on the rock-hard sand along the Florida beach. Stock car races were mostly held on small dirt tracks until the late 1950s, when Bill France built the Daytona International Speedway. The two-and-a-half-mile track had banked curves and a huge grandstand.

Drivers wait for a stock car race to begin at Daytona Beach, Florida, in 1956. (Associated Press)

The first Daytona 500 was held in 1959 and was won by Lee Petty, Richard Petty's father and Kyle Petty's grandfather. Forty-two thousand fans showed up for that first race. The next year, 70,000 showed up—and the crowds have been growing ever since.

School Days

During Jeff's second day at Buck Baker's racing school, the school received visits from car-owner Hugh Connerty, who was looking for a driver. He liked what he saw in Jeff. (Although some drivers own their own race cars, in most cases the boss is the person who owns the car. The driver and everyone else on the team works for the car owner.)

Connerty asked Jeff if he would like to drive for him during the last part of the 1990 season. Connerty's car raced in NASCAR's Busch Grand National division, which was only one level below the major league of stock car racing, the Winston Cup series. The Busch league drove on Saturdays, often at the same track where the Winston Cup boys drove on Sundays.

Jeff said yes. He had accomplished what he had come to the school for. He had landed a job that would make him more money than he had ever seen before and that would put him on TV every Saturday.

On Jeff's last day at Buck Baker's school, Jeff talked his mom into going for a ride with him. She agreed, but only under the condition that he went slow. Jeff agreed and took her through the corners at 150 miles per hour.

When she screamed he said, "Sorry, Mom—but that's as slow as the car will go!"

Welcome to Busch Country

During the 1990 Busch Grand National season Jeff met the man who would become his Winston Cup crew chief: Ray Evernham. Ray had been a crew chief in the International Race of Champions series, and he was looking for a NASCAR job. A friend of his told him that Connerty and Jeff were looking for a crew chief, so they all got together in Charlotte.

"The very first time I saw Jeff," Ray later said, "he looked about 14 or 15 years old. His mother was with him, and he had a briefcase in one hand. He called me Mr. Evernham. He was trying to grow a mustache, not very successfully, and when he opened his briefcase, he had a video game, a cell phone, and racing magazine in it. I asked myself, 'What am I getting into?'"

Ray and Jeff hit it off, but Ray decided to look elsewhere for work and ended up being the crew chief for Alan Kulwicki through the 1991 season.

Jeff's performances in those first few Busch Grand National races were not memorable. He qualified to start on the front row for his first race. A few days before each race the drivers take turns on the track, one at a time, running one lap as fast as they can. The laps are timed and the driver who finishes his trip around the track the fastest gets to start in front, in what is called the *pole position*. The others line up behind him according to their time in their "qualifying" run.

Jeff started in front but crashed soon after the race started. To make matters worse, he smacked into a car driven by Buddy Baker—the son of his NASCAR driving academy instructor, Buck Baker.

What does it feel like to crash in a race car? Jeff once said, "The first feeling is helplessness. You see what's happening, but you know that once you get caught up in the wreck, there's nothing you can do about it. It's like having the legs cut out from under you; you want to keep running, but you can't."

In another race, Jeff failed to qualify altogether. Jeff was not used to competing in races in which the cars actually made contact with one another on the track. Unlike the cars he had previously driven, these cars were enclosed by metal bodies and drivers' strategies sometimes involved bumping and grinding. The drivers call it rubbing. It took some getting used to.

When the season ended, Hugh Connerty was unable to get sponsors and money for the next season.

In the fall of 1990 Jeff returned to midget racing and won his first major championship, the USAC National

Midget Championship. He had just turned 19 years old, the youngest driver ever to win that honor.

Stock car racing paid better than midget racing, however—a lot better—and Jeff's 1990 stock car driving had been impressive enough to get him another job.

In 1991, when Jeff raced his first full season in the Busch division, he did it for a new car owner. The owner was Bill Davis and the car, sponsored by Carolina Ford Dealers, had previously been driven by Mark Martin, who left to run his own team.

John negotiated a deal for Jeff in which he would not receive a salary, but instead get a percentage of the money made by the team. Jeff's driving performance in 1991 was much improved. He finished in second place three times, in the top five on five occasions, and in the top 10 nine times. Jeff qualified fastest, for the pole position, for one race.

The team earned more than $100,000 for the year. Jeff did so well that he won the circuit's Rookie of the Year Award, just barely defeating David Green for that honor.

Ray Comes Aboard

In 1992, for the first time, Jeff drove with Ray Evernham as his crew chief. Ray had left the Alan Kulwicki team and had taken a job with Bill Davis. Jeff's goal had been to win the Rookie of the Year Award during his first year in the Busch

Jeff checks out his car before a race. (Getty Images)

league and to win the driver championship during his second year. He had already made the first part come true, and he came very close to the second part as well. During his second year as a Busch driver, still driving for Bill Davis now in a car sponsored by Nestlé Baby Ruth candy bars, he was near the top in the driver standings throughout the season, but he came up just short, finishing fourth.

In 1992 Jeff raced at the Daytona International Speedway for the first time. Although he started the race at the back of the pack, he passed many cars and was pushing toward the front when his engine gave out on him with 18 laps left.

A week later in Rockingham, Jeff qualified fastest and started on the pole and then finished ninth in the race. At one point during the season, Jeff won the pole for three straight races and finished in the top 10 for two of them.

Jeff got his first win in the Busch series at the Atlanta Motor Speedway that year. He was so overcome with emotion that he had difficulty running the last lap because his eyes were tearing up.

Things were looking up. Jeff says that the difference was his crew chief, Ray Evernham, whom he describes as a "natural-born leader."

4

RAINBOW WARRIORS

Because the Busch league and Winston Cup often shared the same track for the weekend, the top owners in the sport had plenty of opportunity to watch Jeff race. During the 1992 season, Jeff was spotted by car-owner Rick Hendrick. In fact, Hendrick was watching when Jeff took the *checkered flag* in Atlanta and won his first Busch race. (The checkered flag is waved when the winning car crosses the finish line at the end of the race.)

Rick was a 42-year-old former speedboat driver and one of the founders of the National Basketball Association (NBA) team the Charlotte Hornets. He was also one of the first Winston Cup owners who ran a multi-team operation. That is, he owned more than one car in the same race.

Rick spotted Jeff right away because he was driving harder into the corners than the other drivers.

"I said, 'Let's watch this guy a minute, because he's about to bust his butt.' But he never did. . . .'" Rick later recalled. Rick learned from Jeff's roommate, Andy Graves, that Jeff might be available to switch owners at the end of the season.

Andy told Jeff that Rick wanted him to call him, but Jeff thought his roomie was joking and he did not make the call.

Actually, Rick Hendrick was not the only car owner who had been watching the 22-year-old's impressive driving performance during his second year in the Busch league. Two legendary drivers-turned-owners—Junior Johnson and Cale Yarborough—also had their eye on Jeff. In addition to them, Bill Davis, Jeff's Busch owner, had told Jeff that he was trying to put together a Winston Cup team, and that if he did, he would of course want Jeff to be the driver.

Finally, Andy convinced Jeff that Rick Hendrick really wanted him to call. When Jeff made the call and Rick asked him to be his driver, Jeff leaped at the opportunity.

Bill Davis was upset about Jeff leaving him. There were newspaper stories criticizing Jeff's lack of loyalty.

"Bill Davis had been good to me, but sometimes you have to separate friendship and business," Jeff later said. "I realized that if I was going to win a lot of championships, I had to align myself with the best. Rick was that guy."

Hendrick Does His Homework

Late in the 1992 season Jeff signed a contract to drive for Hendrick Motorsports. Hendrick—who was from Charlotte, North Carolina—was one of the biggest car dealers in the United States. And he was not one to make a snap judgment. Before he decided to sign Jeff as his new driver he did a lot of research. He not only watched Jeff drive, but he talked to people who had been close to Jeff through the years. He saw in Jeff as close to a sure thing as there can be in racing. Rick could tell that Jeff was a future superstar.

Most car owners put together a team and then find a driver. But Rick did things a little differently. He signed the driver first, then went out and found a car, a sponsor, and a crew.

Jeff's crew chief turned out to be Ray Evernham, who signed with Hendrick soon after Jeff. A deal to drive a Chevrolet car quickly followed. The new Winston Cup car and team was Rick's third; this was the first time a single owner had run three teams at once. Rick's other two drivers were Ricky Rudd and Ken Schrader. (Over the years Jeff's teammates would change.)

There was concern among fans that multiple-team owners would affect races. What if, they asked, two teammates were racing for a victory? Would the owner order that the driver who needed the win the most be allowed to finish first?

About those concerns, Jeff said, "Those who broached that subject didn't understand the competitive nature of racing. I'm going to race my teammate just as hard as I would anybody else. If anybody thought otherwise, they didn't know me very well."

Jeff would be driving the DuPont Chevrolet. The number 24 was painted on the side and the top of his car in large numerals so it could be clearly read by the scorekeepers at the start-finish line. While Chevrolet was the manufacturer of the car, DuPont Automotive Finishes was the car's sponsor (the company that pays the bills).

DuPont made paints, so the car received a multicolor (red, blue, yellow, and green) paint job that made it stand out in the pack. Because of Jeff's sponsor and the wildly colorful paint job on his car, Jeff's team quickly became known as the "Rainbow Warriors."

Team Effort

In racing, the driver is just one part of a large team effort. Jeff's teammates included the crew chief, who is like the manager on a baseball team or the head coach of a football team. The crew chief works for the team owner, but gets to tell everyone else what to do. It is the crew chief's job to make sure that everything goes smoothly, before, during, and after the race.

One of the things that makes the NASCAR season so interesting is that the races are run on a variety of tracks. Some are two-and-a-half miles around, with steep banks on the corners—which allow drivers more speed—and long straightaways. Others are flat. Some are smaller and force the driver to bump the whole way through heavy traffic. Some are called "road" courses, and feature left- and right-hand turns, as well as uphill and downhill sections. Different cars are used for each type of track. Each type of car has its own parts and tools. Different shock absorbers and springs are used depending on race conditions. Depending on the weather and condition of the track, cars must be

The pit crew prepares the car for racing before the race and makes any necessary repairs or refuelings needed during the race. (Associated Press)

"set up" differently—and it is the crew chief's job to know how each car should be set up for the race.

Then there is the *pit crew*. They are the people who make sure that the car is ready to go before the race, and that is has enough fuel and fresh tires during the race. If something goes wrong with the car during the race, it is the pit crew's job to fix it as fast as possible and to get the car and driver back out on the track. Obviously, when it comes to a sport where cars travel faster than 200 miles per hour, every second counts.

The crew member the driver talks to most during a race is the *spotter*. The spotter, from his perch in the infield, lets the driver know when it is OK to pass the car in front of him. (Stock cars do not have rearview mirrors.) He also tells the driver if there is an accident up ahead so that the driver can know as quickly as possible when to hit the brakes or turn the steering wheel to avoid trouble.

Hendrick teams have been very successful over the years, partly because they really do think like a team. Hendrick Motorsports employs 400 people. There are posters on the walls of the 12-building team headquarters in Charlotte, North Carolina, that read

Together

Everyone

Achieves

More

Where Are the Doors?

Stock cars are built to look just like a car your family might own. But on the inside, stock cars are very different from the automobiles that most people drive.

The headlights are decals. There are no doors. The driver has to climb in and out of the driver-side window. Actually, it's the opening where the driver's side window would nor- mally be. There is no window. Netting covers the opening to keep debris from flying into the car and hitting the driver.

Each part of the car is built by the car owner's shop. The pieces are all built according to NASCAR rules. NASCAR uses Chevrolets, Fords, and Dodges in its races, but they all look alike because the body (the car's outer shell) of each type is built from the same mold. Each part is tested many times to make sure it does not break any NASCAR rules.

The rules are meant to keep the cars as similar to each other as possible. That way the race is between drivers, not between engineers and mechanics. Without the rules, the designer of the best car would win the race. As it exists now, races are won by the car with the best driver, and that's the way NASCAR wants it to be.

All of the parts are also tested to make sure they will not break at a key moment and put the driver at risk of injury. The most obvious difference between the stock car and the family car is the engine. The race car engine is much more powerful, enabling the car to go 220 mph.

All unnecessary parts have been taken out of the stock car. As Jeff says, "There isn't even a speedometer. When you've been racing as long as I have, your butt tells you how fast you are going."

Jeff quickly learned that the hardest part of driving a stock car was the heat. Because the cars have a roof, it gets very hot inside the driver's compartment. The temperature in the driver's seat during a race can be as high as 120°F.

To keep drivers from overheating or getting dizzy from breathing too much carbon monoxide, there is an air hose that pumps fresh air inside the driver's helmet. There is also a water hose in case he gets thirsty. Also inside the helmet are a microphone and a speaker so the driver can talk to his crew during the race.

Winston Cup Debut

Jeff's first Winston Cup race was the 500-mile race at the Atlanta Motor Speedway on November 15, 1992—the last race of the 1992 season. It was also the final Winston Cup race for the legendary "King" Richard Petty, who holds the all-time record for most Winston Cup victories. Petty took the checkered flag 200 times, a record that may never be broken.

Jeff's performance that day at Atlanta did nothing to make headlines. He started 21st and managed to work his way through the pack toward the front until he spun out about halfway through the race and finished 31st. Looking at it from today, it would seem that on that day Richard Petty passed the torch (or maybe the crown) to the new kid.

"To have made my Winston Cup debut at the King's final race was a thrill," Jeff said.

Of all Jeff's transitions, the move up from the Busch league to Winston Cup went the smoothest. Winston Cup cars are more powerful, but they are similar otherwise. Speaking of his new race car, Jeff said, "I immediately felt comfortable in the car."

"How do I get to victory lane?"

As the 1993 Winston Cup season prepared to get under way, Jeff set three goals for himself. First of all, he wanted to win the Rookie of the Year, just as he had in the Busch division. He wanted to finish in the top 10 in the driver standings. And, he wanted to win at least one race.

The Winston Cup season starts at Daytona for two straight weekends of events, the last of which is the biggest stock car race of them all, the Daytona 500. (Big-league stock car racing is organized differently from just about any other sport. Baseball ends its season with its biggest event, the World Series. Football, of course, saves its Super Bowl for last. But NASCAR has its biggest event of the year first. Each season begins with the Daytona 500, the granddaddy of all stock car races.)

To determine who starts at the front of the pack in the Daytona 500, there are two 125-mile qualifier races, plus a qualifying lap is run. The winners of the two races and the car that runs the fastest lap start in the top three spots. Jeff wanted to do well so that he would not have too many cars to pass during the biggest race of the year. He did better than that. He won one of the 125-mile races.

Jeff became the first rookie in 30 years to win a qualifier race, and he was the youngest driver ever to win one. The win came so early in Jeff's career, and it came so unexpectedly, that Jeff had to admit that he did not know what to do.

"Uh, how do I get to victory lane?" he asked his crew chief through the walkie-talkie inside his helmet.

Ray Evernham was pleased to give him instructions on where he needed to go to receive his trophy and the customary kiss from the beauty queen. Little did Jeff know that the kiss would end up changing his life.

Brooke

A funny thing happened to Jeff in victory lane after that first win at Daytona in 1993: He fell in love.

It is a racing custom that the winner of the race gets a kiss from a beauty queen. After Winston Cup races, Miss Winston gives out the smooch. In 1993 the newly crowned

Miss Winston was Brooke Sealey of Winston-Salem, North Carolina. For Jeff and Brooke it was love at first sight. Both knew that, with sparks flying, one kiss on victory lane was the start of something special.

Brooke and Jeff had to be careful, however. There are rules against the drivers dating the beauty queen, so Jeff and Brooke had to keep their relationship a secret for a time. Although driver Kyle Petty caught them out on a date once, Jeff and Brooke's relationship was not made public until they announced their engagement. After that, they were seldom seen apart. She was there when he got into his race car, and there when he got out.

Although Jeff was not very religious, Brooke was. Before long, Jeff was going to church every Sunday and taking part in the Bible studies program that NASCAR makes available to its drivers.

Jeff and Brooke were married on Thanksgiving weekend 1994 in Charlotte. Soon after that Jeff made a series of radio, TV, and print ads for religious causes.

The ad in *Reader's Digest* read: "When you're flying around a track at 180 mph, danger is always there beside you. But in every race I've ever run, in spite of the danger, I've never been afraid. Because deep inside me there's something greater than fear driving me—and that's my personal relationship with God."

Daytona 500

A week after getting that first kiss from Brooke, Jeff raced for the first time in stock car's biggest event, the Daytona 500. Because of his win in the smaller, 125-mile race, he got to start third, on the inside of the second row, for the big race.

On his rear fender was a special stripe that had to be on all cars driven by rookies. Jeff did not drive like a rookie, though. Once the race started Jeff became the first rookie to lead the first lap of the Daytona 500.

With only three laps left to go, Jeff was in second place, with only Dale Earnhardt Sr. in front of him. As the race neared its end, Dale Jarrett passed both Earnhardt and Gordon to win the race.

Jeff finished in fifth place, a solid performance that made his owner and crew chief very happy.

Rookie of the Year—Again

The Charlotte racetrack, the track closest to Hendrick headquarters, was good to Jeff that first year. In the spring race he started in 21st position but passed his way to the front and finished second, his best finish in a Winston Cup race so far. In the autumn race at the same track, he qualified with the fastest time and won his first pole position.

Jeff also finished second in the Michigan race that year. Only Ricky Rudd was faster.

Jeff poses with Dale Earnhardt Sr. after the 1993 Winston Cup. Earnhardt won the championship, and Jeff was named Rookie of the Year. (Associated Press)

After that race Jeff told the press, "The car was awesome the last 100 laps, and I felt we really had a chance of winning the race. We just needed a little luck. I was running down Ricky. I think I could have made a winning move on him if I'd had another lap."

That was pretty cocky talk for a rookie. The veteran drivers and many fans thought that rookies should be seen and not heard.

"I got a little arrogant," Jeff later admitted.

During his rookie season, Jeff only managed to make one of the three goals he had set for himself. He was named the Winston Cup Rookie of the Year for 1993. In fact, he became the first driver to be named top rookie in both the Busch and Winston Cup circuits.

He did not make the top 10 in drivers' standings however, finishing 14th. And, with the exception of the Daytona qualifier, he did not win a race, second place being his best finish. As preparation for the 1994 season began, there was plenty of room for improvement.

Winning and Losing in the Pits

Jeff's first NASCAR race of the 1994 season was the Busch Clash. To qualify for the race, a driver has to have won a pole in a Winston Cup race during the previous season.

The race is held as part of Speedweek, kicking off the season at Daytona. It is not an official Winston Cup race, but it does feature all of the top names in stock car racing and is shown on national TV.

Jeff spent much of the latter part of the race in third place, behind Dale Earnhardt Sr. and Brett Bodine. But, as the race neared its end, Jeff found a little extra speed in his car and flew by Bodine and Earnhardt to take the victory.

He had now finished first in two NASCAR races, a 125-mile qualifier and the Busch Clash, both Daytona races—but neither win had come in an official Winston Cup race.

At the 1994 Daytona 500, Jeff improved slightly on his previous year's performance. During his rookie season he finished fifth. In 1994 he finished fourth. That would have been considered a great day by most drivers, but not by Jeff. He was beginning to get frustrated. He really wanted to win a Winston Cup race.

It looked like victory would be his at that year's race in Richmond. Jeff had the fastest car. He had been dominating the race. Then an error in the pits cost him the win.

Jeff came in for gas and new tires, but drove out of his pit before his left front tire was all the way on. The mistake cost him, although he still ended up finishing third in the race.

His wait for a Winston Cup victory did not end until that May. At the end of Jeff's first 40 Winston Cup races, he had watched someone else take the checkered flag and win the race. But that streak was broken in his 41st race. And it was broken at what was quickly becoming Jeff's favorite track, the Charlotte Motor Speedway.

The Memorial Day race in Charlotte, the Coca-Cola 600, was the longest race on the schedule. The 600-mile race is so long that it starts during the day and ends under the lights at night. (It is not held earlier so as not to compete with the Indianapolis 500, which always runs on the same day.)

Although a pit stop in Richmond cost Jeff a victory, a pit stop in Charlotte earned him one. The key to victory was Jeff's final pit stop of the race with only 25 laps left.

Ray Evernham took a quick look at Jeff's tires as he rolled to a stop in his pit. The crew chief held up two fingers. So Jeff took on only two new tires rather than four.

It takes less time to change two tires than it does to change four. But, there is a chance that the car will not run as fast because it still has two old tires on it. The two-tire pit stop made the car more difficult to drive, but it got Jeff out of his pit in less than nine seconds.

That turned out to be the difference. Jeff crossed the finish line beneath the waving checkered flag, ahead of veteran fan-favorite Rusty Wallace. Wallace, on his final pit stop, had decided to take on four new tires. Wallace's pit stop lasted more than 17 seconds, eight seconds longer than Gordon's. Eight seconds was the margin of victory.

When Jeff emerged from the cockpit on victory lane, tears were streaming down his face. He told a reporter: "Getting that first win, especially in my own backyard, is a feeling I'll never forget. This is the highest feeling in the world. If there's a higher feeling than this, I don't know what it is. Those last few laps, I was just trying to keep from hitting the wall because of all the tears in my face. On the last lap, I choked up and completely lost it."

Wallace was impressed with the gamble the Gordon team took on its final pit stop.

"I never thought he'd try two tires," Rusty said. "And I never thought it would work. It was a chancy move—a pretty savvy move on their part."

Because of Jeff's win, Hendrick Motorsports was $200,000 richer. There was a quick party and then it was time to move to the next town, to the next racetrack, for the next weekend's race.

5

WONDER BOY

Through most of the 20th century the Indianapolis Motor Speedway, near where Jeff lived as a teenager, was host to only one event per year, the Indianapolis 500, the "Greatest Spectacle in Racing." But in 1994 that changed.

NASCAR convinced the Speedway to allow it to have a Winston Cup race there in August. The track was nicknamed "the Brickyard" because its two-and-a-half mile track was so old that, at one time, it had been laid with bricks.

The track had been paved over years before, with the exception of a one-yard strip on the front stretch, which served as the track's start-finish line. But, other than that, the track remained the same as it was in the 1910s when automobiles were new. It is narrower, flatter, and has sharper turns than the other *superspeedways* used by NASCAR.

The Indianapolis stock car race would be called the Brickyard 400. Finally, America's most popular drivers would race at America's most popular track. It was quite an event and 350,000 screaming fans showed up to see the first running of the Brickyard 400.

The Inaugural Brickyard

Before the race, all 43 starting drivers were lined up along the start-finish line for a commemorative photo. As the pre-race excitement grew, Jeff told a trackside reporter, "To come out of here with a victory would mean more to me than anything in this whole world. I don't even think I can put it into words. I'm just glad to be a part of this thing."

In car racing, the waving of a *green flag* means that the race has begun. In Indianapolis that day, it was 70 degrees and sunny as the green flag fell. Rick Mast led the first lap. Dale Earnhardt Sr. and Mast came together at the start, and Earnhardt bent his car's rear end badly enough to affect his handling. He slammed the wall in turn four.

Jeff passed Mast to take the lead. Jeff was under orders from his pit to not show his entire hand, to hold back, and to not pull away from the pack.

Debris in the first turn brought out yellow (the caution flag) soon thereafter. This was a huge break for Earnhardt, since it gave him time to take care of his problems.

Jimmy Spencer was the first car to fall out of the race when he smacked the wall hard on lap 10, bringing out the second yellow. Spencer exited the car hesitantly, favoring his right arm, and climbed into the ambulance. Spencer later said he aggravated a shoulder injury he suffered earlier in the year in a short-track practice incident. He was sent to Methodist Hospital for X rays.

Cars with *pushes*—that is, cars that wanted to go straight even when the driver was trying to turn left—were a problem. Driver-owner Geoff Bodine called into his crew saying, "Man, this thing is pushing like a dump truck."

It was Gordon, Geoff Bodine, Mast, and Bill Elliott leading a single-file pack when racing returned. Bodine passed Gordon to take the lead on lap 24.

The first pit stops came on lap 32. Many drivers, not used to the track, appeared tentative coming onto pit road. Geoff Bodine's brother Todd briefly led the race until he suffered a slow pit stop, during which a jack fell off many times.

Gordon had a problem on his pit stop, too. Another jack fell off, and Jeff complained of hearing a vibration in the car. The lead changed several times as cars made pit stops, but, when the shake-up was through, Gordon was back in the lead.

On a later pit stop, Jeff Gordon and Geoff Bodine made contact coming into the pits, which left a big tire mark on the side of Gordon's car. The rainbow paint job was injured, but everything else was okay and Jeff held his lead through the halfway mark in the race. Gordon and Bodine had the two fastest cars and they exchanged the lead a couple of times.

Then, Geoff Bodine was taken out of the race—by one of his brothers! On lap 100 Geoff and Brett Bodine got into a bumping war going into turn three, and eventually caused a chaotic traffic jam at the mouth of pit road.

Geoff tapped Brett's car on the third turn and Brett, getting brotherly revenge, banged into Geoff coming off turn four. The contact was hard enough to turn Geoff's car around. To avoid the accident, at least a dozen cars bailed into pit road. Brett's car was not harmed in the incident.

With Geoff Bodine out of the race, there did not appear to be anyone on the track who could keep up with Jeff Gordon. Jeff began to run away from the pack. A couple of yellow flags and pit stops tightened things up. With 27 laps to go, Rusty Wallace hit the gas first on a restart and passed Jeff for the lead. But Gordon and Ernie Irvan were right on Wallace's tail, leading to some incredibly close racing until Rusty backed off with a problem—he apparently shied away because of too much traffic—and fell back to sixth place. That left Gordon in front with Irvan right behind him.

Ernie Irvan became the 13th leader of the race by passing Jeff Gordon with 50 miles to the finish. Gordon tucked himself right on his bumper and passed in turn one with 17 laps to go.

With 13 laps remaining, the two leaders had reversed positions, with Irvan right on his bumper. With 12 to go, they exchanged the lead several times running around the track side by side. Irvan settled back in front.

Because of the side-by-side racing, the pack caught them with Brett Bodine, Elliott, Earnhardt, and Wallace pulling up close. When Irvan and Gordon reestablished their *draft,* they again pulled away from the others.

With five laps left, Irvan missed the entrance to turn one with a shredded tire, and Gordon took the lead with a lot of space between himself and Brett Bodine, who was in second place. Irvan went down a lap while getting his tire changed. With Irvan out of the way, Jeff cruised to the checkered flag with a four-car-length lead to become the first winner of the Brickyard 400.

"Oh my God, oh my God, I did it," he screamed via radio to his crew as he crossed the start-finish line. Gordon's average speed was 131.608 mph. The cars raced at speeds much faster than that, but the average speed was slowed by the fact that 25 laps were run under the yellow flag.

In victory lane, Gordon, who had only turned 23 the Thursday before the race, said, "We had a great car all day long. The only car I was worried about was that number 7 car [Ernie Irvan], and then I saw he had his misfortune.

Jeff was the winner at the first Brickyard 400, held in 1994.
(Associated Press)

Ernie did a good job of loosening me up there for a while. Ernie Irvan drove a nice clean race, we didn't have to worry about anything."

For his winning effort at Indianapolis, Jeff was given a check for $613,000, the largest check ever handed out for a NASCAR event. To celebrate, Jeff and Brooke had pizza and watched a replay of the race on TV.

Experts were now calling Jeff the most talented driver on the NASCAR circuit. The fans had mixed reviews. Those who preferred to cheer for other drivers did not like the new upstart joining the circuit and taking glory away from their heroes right away.

Where's His Drawl?

Because most NASCAR drivers and many of the fans come from the American South, some of the folks in the grandstand did not like the fact that Jeff was from California and Indiana, where people do not speak with a Southern drawl. Other fans disliked him because he did not share many of the fans' other common interests, such as hunting and fishing.

But other NASCAR lovers immediately turned into Jeff Gordon fans. One thing was certain: With his big win at the Brickyard, Jeff had become a superstar. The Hendrick team was more than a half-a-million dollars richer and Jeff Gordon had become a household name.

There may have been some fans who were slow to warm up to Jeff, but that was not true of his fellow drivers. When your job includes driving at 200 miles per hour bumper to bumper with other drivers, respecting and trusting your colleagues is very important. And the other NASCAR drivers respected and trusted Jeff right away.

One of the first drivers to speak out about Jeff was NASCAR veteran Mark Martin. Martin said, "I approve of him, the way he lives his life, the way he conducts himself, and everything else. If some fans don't like Jeff Gordon they should just imagine how a different personality could be in his situation. It hurts me to hear him booed because he's good."

In 1994 Jeff finished eighth in the Winston Cup points standings. Dale Earnhardt won the championship for the second year running. Because of the big check he had received at the Brickyard 400, Jeff finished third in money earned.

Jeff later said, "We had too many races we did not finish to be competitive for the championship. Ten times we crashed, blew an engine, lost a transmission, or otherwise had mechanical failures that blew us out of the race." (A malfunctioning engine at 200 mph can actually explode with a huge puff of smoke. That's called "blowing an engine.")

With their newfound riches, Jeff and Brooke purchased a mansion on the beach near Boca Raton, Florida. The huge house had a great front yard: The 23,000-square-foot home came with 125 feet of beachfront on Highland Beach. The mansion came with its own elevator, wine cellar, and theater. By this time Jeff had also acquired a new nickname among NASCAR fans: Wonder Boy.

Finishing What They Started

The NASCAR Winston Cup championship is based on a points system. The winner of a race scores the most points, second place scores a few less points, a little less for third place, and so on down the line.

At the end of the year when all of the races have been run, the points are added up and the driver with the most points wins the championship. It is possible for a driver to become the champion without actually winning a race.

A driver who regularly finishes in the top five will end up with more points than will a driver who wins several races but fails to finish several others.

In 1995 the main goal of Jeff's team was to cut down on their "did not finishes." They aimed to finish what they started. Without finishing close to all of the races on the schedule, it was next to impossible to win the points championship.

By 1995, Jeff's third season racing on the Winston Cup circuit, he had only one goal: win the championship. He was going to have to do it in a new kind of car. Like all of the drivers of Chevys in Winston Cup, Jeff was switching from the Lumina to the Monte Carlo for the 1995 season.

Jeff qualified to start in fourth position for the 1995 Daytona 500, on the outside of the second row. Jeff led the race for 50 laps, but another pit mistake cost him the race, again involving the left front tire. Jeff hit the gas before the tire was all the way on. The tire came completely off and the car sustained front-end damage.

"It's a shame. We had it, and we gave it away," Ray Evernham said after the race.

Intimidator in the Rearview Mirror

With that mistake out of its system, Jeff's team got into a groove in 1995. The week after Daytona, Jeff won in Rockingham, North Carolina. Two weeks later he again finished first in Bristol, Tennessee.

Throughout 1995 it was a two-man race: Jeff and two-time defending champion Dale Earnhardt Sr., known to racing fans as "the Intimidator." That NASCAR season started in February at Daytona and ended in October at Atlanta.

During the spring and most of the summer, it was clearly Jeff's year. By Labor Day, Jeff had built up a 300-point lead over the second-place Earnhardt.

It looked like Jeff was going to cruise to the championship. But Jeff knew that when Dale Earnhardt was in pursuit, a driver could not relax.

Sure enough, Earnhardt began to charge hard, winning race after race. Each week Jeff's point lead shrunk a little. Going into the final race of the season Gordon had a small 34-point lead over Earnhardt.

But Jeff finished ahead of Dale in the last race. At age 24, Jeff Gordon became the youngest Winston Cup champion of the modern era. (The "modern era" began in 1959 with the first running of the Daytona 500.) The only driver to win the championship at a younger age was Bill Rexford, who was 22 when he took the honors in 1950. It was also the first Winston Cup championship for Hendrick Motorsports. Jeff's championship had earned Hendrick Motorsports $4.3 million.

During the season, Jeff won seven races in all. And he started on the pole eight times. He had finished in the top three 16 times. (Earnhardt had also finished in the top three 16 times, but had won only five events.)

Jeff was officially named NASCAR's top driver that December at the Waldorf-Astoria hotel in New York City. Accepting his award, he toasted all of those whom he wanted to thank. He toasted Earnhardt for being such a tough competitor, Ray Evernham for being a great crew chief, Hendrick Motorsports, and all of the Rainbow

Warriors. Finally, he raised a glass to John and Carol Bickford for being such great parents, and for all of the sacrifices they made to get him to where he was—at the top of the stock car world.

A Week in the Life

One of the things that makes Jeff a winner is his dedication to his racing schedule. The following is a typical week for Jeff during racing season. Races are usually held on Sunday, so Monday is his day off. He uses this day to relax and catch up on personal business.

In addition to his responsibilities regarding setting up the car and strategy for the upcoming race, Jeff has other weekly duties as well. On Tuesdays and Wednesdays he makes appearances for his sponsors, visiting guests and promoting the products that help his team pay the bills.

Jeff says, "I've always done my best to make sure that my sponsors are happy with their investment."

Jeff arrives at the track on Thursday. While some team members ride the bus from track to track, Jeff does not. He has a private plane and flies into the nearest airport. From there, someone from the team picks him up and drives him to the racetrack.

The NASCAR season lasts for eight months. During that time Jeff sleeps three nights a week—Thursday, Friday, and Saturday—on the team bus.

On the Friday before the race, qualifying is held. Each team runs its car once around that week's track against a clock. The cars then start the race in the order they qualify, from fastest to slowest. The pole-sitter (the driver with the best time) not only gets to start on the inside of the front row, but gets to choose which pit along pit road he wants.

Saturday is practice day. The driver runs laps and tries to get comfortable with the track, while the crew fine-tunes the car to make sure the setup is just right.

Race day starts with a drivers' meeting, during which safety matters and new rules are discussed. After that, many of the drivers, including Jeff, go to a chapel service held each week at the track, wherever the track may be. After the service, Jeff heads back to his transporter—the huge tractor-trailer that carries the car, the auto shop, and the Hendrick Motorsports office-on-wheels from track to track.

This short walk sometimes turns into a hard journey. There are usually many fans between the chapel and the transporter, all of who want to say hi to Jeff or maybe get his autograph.

A half hour before the race starts, the drivers are intro-duced to the crowd. Forty-three cars start the race (races are usually, but not always, held on Sunday). As the driv-ers are being introduced, the cars are parked on pit road.

Following introductions, the drivers climb into their cars. They run through a series of checks to make sure everything is operating properly. Then someone, usually a guest celebrity, says, "Gentlemen, start your engines." The roar of 43 racing engines firing at once is thunderous.

Running in rows of two, the cars parade around the track to warm up their tires, following behind the pace car, which keeps them from going too fast. When the cars are warmed up, and as they approach the start-finish line, the starter waves a green flag and the race is on.

6

JEFF GORDON INC.

In 1996 Jeff won 10 races, as opposed to the seven he had won the previous year. He won twice as many races as any other Winston Cup driver—but he did not win the championship. He finished second to his Hendrick Motorsports teammate Terry Labonte, who had won only two races. But Labonte finished in the top five more often, and in the top 10 more often. In fact, Labonte had finished in the top 10 in 27 of the 31 races that year. When the points were added up, Labonte had a 37-point lead over his teammate.

Handling Wealth and Fame

Being a middle-class kid, Jeff had no idea what to do with all of the money he was suddenly making. For a while his parents, Carol and John, tried to manage all of Jeff's money, but it eventually became too much of a job.

Jeff hired professionals to handle his finances for him. A banker from North Carolina named Bob Brannan became the manager of the brand-new company Jeff Gordon Inc.

Jeff saved and invested money, of course, but he spent some of it too. Along with the big house on the beach, he purchased a midsize private jet called the Falcon 200, so that he and Brooke would not have to deal with long lines at airports anymore.

Jeff began to make friends with celebrities from other sports. Among them was Charles Barkley, who was then playing for the Phoenix Suns. Jeff learned from Charles the importance of being relaxed when dealing with fans. He learned that being relaxed and being himself immediately put the fans at ease.

Jeff never misses an opportunity to visit hospitals where he tries to cheer up both adults and children who are seriously ill. "It's very heartbreaking," Jeff says about those visits. "Because here you are living a life that couldn't get any better and you're seeing somebody whose life almost couldn't get any worse. If there is any way I can help, if there is anything I can do, if it's an inspiration to somebody because he or she is a fan of mine, that's the easiest thing I could ever do."

Still, some fans continued to boo him. Jeff says he understands why.

"It just means that they're fans of other drivers," he says, shrugging it off. "They're booing you because either you're winning too much or you're doing something you're not supposed to. I have a smile on my face because I must be doing something right. You listen to how much noise is being made when you are introduced, and you want the loudest and longest noise. Some of them are booing, some of them are cheering, and some of them don't know which way to go."

Daytona Glory

Bad news struck the Hendrick team near the end of 1996. Rick Hendrick, the team owner, was suffering from leukemia. When Jeff heard the news, he went to churches and hospitals where he signed autographs and encouraged people to sign up to be bone marrow donors.

From then on, Rick was too sick to be the normal hands-on owner that the team had grown used to. Despite this bad news, the following season could not have gotten off to a better start for the Rainbow Warriors. On February 16, 1997, Jeff won the Daytona 500.

The 42-car field, with rookie Mike Skinner on the pole, featured 22 Fords, 12 Chevrolets, and seven Pontiacs. The cash prize (or purse, as it is called) was a cool $4.3 million. It was just the kind of race that NASCAR fans love: lots of speed, lots of crashes, and few injuries. An exciting finish would have been nice, but you can't have everything.

On the ninth lap Robert Pressley took a wild ride. He lost control coming out of turn four and his car went airborne. It spun on its nose like a figure skater and then crashed down wheels first. Pressley was taken to the hospital for X rays on a sore hip.

Then, on lap 48, Jimmy Spencer got too close to the wall and lost control, taking Geoff Bodine and Derrike Cope with him. Because of the accident, Spencer lost his brakes and went careening into the pits. As Spencer's pit crew got into position to change the tires, Spencer was yelling to his crew that he had no brakes. He hit his jackman (a member of the pit crew) who was running into position. Unbelievably, the jackman got back up and finished the pit stop before limping back to the pit wall.

On lap 56, Ernie Irvan took over the lead, with Jeff right behind him. A lap later, Jeff briefly took the lead, but for the most part Jeff was content to let other drivers run out in front. While other cars led the way, Jeff concentrated on staying out of trouble and remaining close to the lead.

On lap 90 there was another crash, this one between Steve Grissom and Ken Schrader, who collided while racing for eighth position. Schrader hit Grissom's car in the rear end, and then both their cars went into the grass

Jeff's car (number 24) zooms across the finish line to win the 1997 Daytona 500. (Associated Press)

infield. Then they spun in sync back across the track, each slapping the outer wall at the same time. They both hit that wall driver-side first and then slid, still in perfect sync, across the track a second time and into the infield where they came to a stop.

Bill Elliott and Dale Earnhardt Sr. were running in first and second place, respectively, with 40 miles to go. Jeff was a close third. On lap 188, with 12 laps remaining, Earnhardt wiggled too close to the wall while Gordon was trying to pass. Dale Jarrett touched Earnhardt, sending the number 3 car tumbling out of control. Earnhardt flipped right over Ernie Irvan's car. This contact ripped off Irvan's hood, which spun like a Frisbee into the grandstand, breaking a woman's arm and injuring a man's knee. Earnhardt's car flipped over and landed on all four wheels. As Earnhardt was getting into the ambulance, he noticed that his car still had all four wheels intact. He asked the wrecker to see if the engine would still work. It started, so Earnhardt bolted out of the ambulance and drove his car back to the pits. The crew then taped the car back together and Earnhardt came back out on lap 193.

On lap 195, Gordon took over the lead by going all the way to the bottom of the track, taking his teammates Terry Labonte and Ricky Craven with him.

The following lap, Bobby Hamilton lost control and eight other cars were caught up in the wreck. The NASCAR crews tried to get the track cleared for a one-lap shootout, but there was not enough time. So, with the yellow flag still waving for the last two laps, Jeff Gordon just cruised to his first Daytona 500 victory.

The Hendrick teams took the first three spots. Gordon, Labonte, and Craven came in first, second, third, respectively. Bill Elliott finished fourth.

As Gordon headed toward victory lane, one of his crew members threw a cellular phone into the car and Jeff called Rick Hendrick with news of his win. Hendrick had stayed home in Charlotte to undergo cancer treatments.

Jeff jumps in the air from the roof of his car after winning the 1997 Winston Cup. (Associated Press)

Jeff Gordon, 25 years old, was the youngest driver to ever win the Daytona 500.

Thus began one of the greatest seasons stock car racing has ever seen. In April, Jeff took the checkered flag in one of the most exciting races in NASCAR history. The race was the Food City 500, and Jeff and Rusty Wallace came toward the finish line side by side. They bumped each other as they went, "swapping paint," as they say. But it was Gordon who crossed the line first for the win.

The next weekend Jeff managed to overcome adversity to again finish first. In this race he spun out early, but still managed to come from behind to pass Bobby Hamilton for the lead on the last lap. Before the season was over, Jeff won 10 races and the Winston Cup championship.

7

THE GREATEST SEASON EVER

If Jeff's 1997 season was one of the greatest seasons ever for a stock car driver, then Jeff's 1998 season was *the* greatest ever. After winning 10 races each during the 1996 and 1997 seasons, Jeff did even better than that in 1998, taking the checkered flag 13 times. At one point during the season he won four races in a row. He started seven races on the pole and earned more than $9 million.

At the end of the season, Jeff had completed a four-year stretch in which he had not finished worse than second in the points standings. During the years 1995–98, Jeff won 40 Winston Cup races.

In 127 races, he finished in the top 10 spots 98 times. During that stretch he led 8,541 laps, more than the second- and third-place drivers combined.

Folks were starting to wonder what it was that gave Jeff and his team such an edge. Some thought they were cheating. Others thought the answer was Jeff's size. Jeff only weighs 150 pounds, and that's a good 50 pounds less than some of the drivers. That 50-pound difference may not seem like much inside a car that weighs almost two tons, but over a whole afternoon of racing it could give him just enough edge to win the race.

Because of this, NASCAR changed its rules. The rule used to be that all cars had to be weighed before the race to make sure they were the same. This was done while the driver was elsewhere. Now the cars were weighed with the driver sitting in them, so small drivers no longer have an advantage over larger ones. (If a car is underweight, weight is added so that all cars weigh the same.)

Changes

For four years the Rainbow Warriors had been riding a wave of good fortune. Everything went their way. Then, in 1999, things began to fall apart. Rick Hendrick was still battling his illness and was away from the track most of the time.

Jeff started the 1999 season by qualifying on the pole for the Daytona 500. In the race itself, things got off to a rocky start. Jeff was penalized 15 seconds by track officials when it was determined that he had too many members of his pit crew working on his car at once during a pit stop. The rule says that there can only be seven crew members "over the wall," that is, working on the car in the pit, at once. In what Jeff later called a "bonehead mistake," eight crew members worked on his car on his first pit stop during the biggest race of the year.

Taking his time and looking for passing opportunities, Jeff got back those 15 seconds and slowly pushed his way back toward the front. With 11 laps left he was in third place.

In some of the wildest racing Daytona has ever seen, Jeff, Rusty Wallace, and Mike Skinner drove several laps side by side, with Dale Earnhardt Sr. and Ricky Rudd approaching fast.

Jeff made a breathtaking move on the track, pulling ahead and diving to the inside. He came within inches of causing a major crash, but there was no contact and he was in the lead, with Earnhardt on his tail.

Jeff managed to keep Earnhardt from passing him over the last 10 laps and won the 1999 Daytona 500.

About that victory Jeff later said, "Too bad it was the highlight of our season."

The following week in Rockingham, Jeff's car blew an engine and he did not finish. But he returned to the front the week after that with a win in Atlanta. After five races, Jeff had finished in the top five four times.

Then the team traveled to Texas for the sixth race of the year, which turned out to be the most painful Jeff had ever experienced. During the race Jeff's car blew a tire and he crashed hard into the wall, bruising his ribs.

Six more times that summer Jeff failed to finish a race because he crashed or the car broke down. It was clear that Jeff's team was out of the running for the 1999 points championship.

During the season, Jeff's longtime crew chief Ray Evernham decided that he wanted to be more than just a crew chief. He wanted to own a race car. He was looking for other opportunities.

In September, in the middle of the season, Ray quit the Rainbow Warriors to become owner of a Dodge Winston Cup car. Ray asked Jeff if he wanted to come with him and be the driver for his new team.

Jeff said no thanks; he would stick with Hendrick Motorsports. Jeff's new crew chief—at least until the end of the season—was Brian Whitesell, a longtime crew member who had been promoted to chief. Brian was the guy who had driven the truck, and he was also the team's timer and chassis technician. He had been the team's top engineer for all three of its championship seasons.

Still, losing Ray was bad news for Jeff. "Ray had been the only crew chief I'd ever had in Winston Cup," Jeff later said. "He was someone I looked to as a younger version of my dad. Ray's decision to leave was as big a personal blow to me as it was a professional hit for our team."

The Rainbow Warriors had been a well-oiled machine. Suddenly it was missing pieces. There were those who thought that Gordon could not win without Evernham, that it had been Evernham and not Gordon who had given the Rainbow Warriors their edge over the competition.

In Jeff's first race with Brian as crew chief, in Dover, Delaware, he finished 17th. "I couldn't help questioning our future," Jeff later recalled.

Getting Rick Back to Victory Lane

The most emotional win of the year for Jeff came at the UAW-GM 500 race at Lowe's Motor Speedway in Charlotte, North Carolina, on October 11, 1999. That was because this was the first race of the year that Rick Hendrick had been strong enough to attend in person.

After the race Jeff said, "I've been waiting for this day for a long time, waiting to get Rick Hendrick back to victory lane. I knew it was going to happen. I just didn't know when. For me to be able to take Rick Hendrick to victory lane today was very emotional and probably one of the highlights not only of this year, but of my career."

The victory was emotional, but it was not easy. Jeff had not had a good qualifying run and was forced to start the race in 22nd position. He worked his way patiently through the pack and did not take the lead until there were less than 10 miles left in the race.

The biggest obstacle Jeff had to overcome was the weather. The race had been scheduled for Sunday, but it had been rained out. The race was held on Monday, when the sun came out. The rain cancellation was lucky for Hendrick Motorsports, however. On Sunday, Rick had felt too sick to go to the track. If it had not rained, he would have missed Jeff's victory. So it all worked out for the best.

That same month, at the Martinsville Speedway in Virginia, it was Brian Whitesell's strategy that led to a win. There was an accident late in the race and all of the other leaders made pit stops to change tires—all except Jeff. He stayed out on the track and built up a lead while the others were getting "fresh rubber."

The last few laps were exciting as Dale Earnhardt Sr. came charging toward the front. But Jeff refused to allow the Intimidator to pass.

After the race Jeff told reporters that his new crew chief was responsible for the victory. "It was a great call," Jeff said of Whitesell's decision to keep the car on the track. "He said that we ought to stay out. I looked around to see what the other guys were going to do. Even though I knew they were coming in [to the pits], I think it was the right call. It just worked out perfectly."

Jeff ended up winning seven races in 1999. It was the first time in four years that he had not won at least 10 times, but he still had more victories than did any other driver on the circuit. But he did not win the championship. That went to Bobby Labonte, the brother of Jeff's teammate Terry.

So Long, Pit Crew

The feeling that the Rainbow Warriors were falling apart became worse for Jeff following the last race of the 1999 season. The pit crew quit. Without Ray, they did not think the team had a chance of winning, so they left.

Talking to a reporter, Jeff tried to stay upbeat: "I'm looking forward to the off-season to get this team back on track," he said. "We've got to make a lot of adjustments over the off-season because we lost our pit crew and Ray [Evernham] and a couple of other guys. We weren't really prepared at the end of the season. If you're not perfect, you're not going to be able to win races."

There was work to be done. A full-time crew chief needed to be found. A new pit crew would need to be hired. (Brian would become the team manager.) But Jeff decided he was not going anywhere. At the end of the season Jeff signed a lifetime contract to drive for Rick Hendrick. A couple of months later came the best news of all. After years of treatment, Rick's leukemia was in remission.

Jeff Gordon Boulevard

The people in Jeff's hometown of Pittsboro, Indiana, were proud of his success. During the summer of 1999 the highway formerly named Country Road 275 had an official name change. At a ceremony that Jeff attended, the road became known as Jeff Gordon Boulevard. In Pittsboro, it is possible to get just about anything with a picture of Jeff on it, from baseball caps to baby shoes.

Even people in Pittsboro who aren't racing fans are Gordon fans because of his boyish good looks and pleasant manner. If his success continues do not be surprised if one day the town itself changes its name to Gordonboro.

Helping Others

During the off-season between the 1999 and 2000 seasons, Jeff went to work putting together an organization designed to help the less fortunate. In 1999 the Jeff Gordon Foundation was formed to raise money for kids who needed help the most.

According to Jeff, "Children and families are the heart and hope of our future. Each child is special and deserves every opportunity for a safe and healthy life. The Jeff Gordon Foundation is dedicated to help support the physical, social, and intellectual needs of children and their families throughout the United States."

8

REBUILDING

Good-natured Robbie Loomis became Jeff's new crew chief in November 1999. Robbie grew up in Florida and learned his skills building race cars in Orlando. In 1988 Petty Enterprises had hired him as a mechanic. In 1991 he became "King" Richard Petty's crew chief. When Petty retired, Robbie stayed on with Petty Enterprises. When Hendrick offered Loomis the job as Jeff's crew chief, Robbie asked Petty for permission. The King gave him his blessing.

"This is a real good opportunity for you. Jeff's a winner," Petty said.

Instead of hiring new people to be his pit crew, it was decided that mechanics from the shop would work weekends as the pit crew. They would have to learn on the job.

With so many changes all happening at once, Jeff did not have high expectations for the 2000 season. It would take a while, he knew, for everything to gel. Jeff and Ray Evernham had learned to communicate without saying a whole lot. Jeff tried that with his new crew chief, Robbie, and, as Jeff later put it, "I saw a lot of blank expressions on Robbie's face."

As the season was about to start Jeff told a pack of reporters, "Right now we have some unknowns as far as working together, but I feel good about the things we are doing. I feel really good about the cars we're building. Our guys could not have done a better job, considering what we've been through."

In private, however, Jeff figured, "We would be lucky to be a middle-of-the-pack team." To make matters even more difficult, Jeff wrecked the car the day before the Daytona 500. He got caught up in a crash that was not his fault and tore up the car's front end. Instead of switching to the backup car, Robbie decided to fix the car in time for the next day's race. The crew worked all night on the repairs.

(Teams are allowed to bring only two cars to the track per driver: the primary car and the backup car. The backup car can be used if the primary car crashes or blows an engine during practice. If a driver qualifies with his primary car and, for whatever reason, must drive the backup car in the race, he has to start from the back of the pack, no matter where he qualified at first.)

The car was ready by race time, but it did not perform well. An oil fitting broke during the race, and although Jeff finished, it was in 34th place.

From Unhappy to Grim

Things were better the next week in Rockingham, but there were still problems. Jeff started the race on the inside of the third row and managed to push his way into the lead briefly. Then there were problems during a pit stop, and Jeff left the stop while the lug nut on one of his wheels was still loose. He had to come back into the pit to have them tightened. He lost the lead and finished 10th. But, as Jeff said, "It wasn't a happy 10th."

Fans along pit road were starting to yell nasty things at Robbie Loomis—things like, "You're ruining Jeff Gordon's career." Robbie tried not to listen, but the comments hurt.

A grim 28th-place finish in Las Vegas followed. Then came a ninth-place finish in Atlanta that perked the crew up. Things really started looking up in Talladega, Alabama, where Jeff won. He won a second time in the Sears Point road course race. It was the sixth-straight road course race Jeff had won—an indication of how well Jeff might have done had he chosen to race in the Formula One Grand Prix circuit, where all of the races are run on road courses.

Jeff's streak of road course wins came to an end that year at Watkins Glen, New York, when Jeff hit a guardrail and lost a lap while repairs were being made. He finished 23rd.

Saturday Night in Richmond

Things got even better at the Saturday night race at Richmond, Virginia. Jeff started in 15th place but took his time and worked toward the front. With 40 laps to go on the three-quarter-mile track, Jeff had pushed into the top five.

He was in second place behind Jeff Burton with 20 laps to go. After a caution period, Gordon passed Burton on the right at the restart and took the lead for the first time in the race.

Gordon then looked in his rearview mirror and saw a familiar sight: The black car of Dale Earnhardt Sr. was on his tail. But Jeff managed to hold the lead and won the race by three-quarters of a second.

"We're back," Jeff said.

During the last 11 races of the year Jeff finished in the top 10 nine times. There were times when the team still did not function perfectly but, as Jeff put it, they were "real, real close."

Tragedy at Daytona

The 2001 season could not have gotten off to a more miserable start. Jeff, who had invested some of his money in Hendricks Motorsports and was now part-owner of his own racing team, started the Daytona 500 in 13th position. Once the race began things fell apart. Although he charged to the lead and appeared to have the fastest car on the track, he was caught in a big crash on lap 177 and finished a dismal 30th.

The outcome of the race became unimportant, however, when racing legend Dale Earnhardt Sr. crashed hard into the wall and was fatally injured during the race's last lap.

After the tragedy Jeff said, "Dale and I were kindred spirits. His death is a terrible blow and a painful reminder of one of the basic truths of our profession: Take nothing for granted when you make your living in a race car."

NASCAR continued under a cloud of grief for the remainder of the season. There were tributes to Earnhardt at every track, and RVs flying black flags with a white number 3 (Earnhardt's number) on them continued to fill the infields.

On the track, the show went on. Jeff and the other drivers drove through their grief. The week after Daytona, Jeff qualified with the fastest time at Rockingham for the Dura Lube 400 and started on the pole.

Before the race Jeff told his team, "You all know we've got a job to do today. But we've got another reason for being here today: to pay tribute to Dale. There's something missing today. I know you feel it. I feel it. We all know what Dale would have wanted us to do."

The weather was a factor in the Rockingham race. Rain stopped the race a couple of times, and it was not finished until Monday morning. Jeff led for the most laps and ended up finishing third.

After the race Jeff told reporters, "This was a tough week for everybody, but at the same time we're kind of a family out here, and it was good to get back out here and go racing."

A Well-Placed Piece of Duct Tape

The situation further improved in the third race of the season in Las Vegas. Although qualifying did not go that well—Jeff started on the outside of the 12th row—Robbie Loomis made several adjustments on the car during the race.

In this high-tech computerized world, sometimes it's still the simple things that separate winners from losers at the racetrack. In this race it was a piece of duct tape that Robbie put on the car's front grille during the race that made the difference. The tape increased the _downforce_—the pressure of the air on a car as it races. Downforce increases with the speed, and can help the car handle better. Jeff led the final lap for his first victory of the year—and he had Robbie Loomis and that piece of duct tape to thank for it.

Following that race Jeff was in second place in the points standings and was clearly a contender for the championship.

The next week, in Atlanta, Jeff finished in what appeared to be a dead heat—a tie—with Kevin Harvick.

Computers showed that Harvick had won the race by .006 of a second, the smallest margin of victory in NASCAR history. The second-place finish, however, was enough to move Gordon into first place in the points standings, the first time he had held that position since the 1999 season.

Jeff had six other victories that year. These included his third victory in the Brickyard 400 at the Indianapolis Motor Speedway, and a road-race win the following week in Watkins Glen.

9/11

Two weeks of racing were postponed due to the terrorist attacks on September 11, 2001. The drivers returned to the track on September 23 in Dover, Delaware, for what Jeff called "the most moving and emotional sporting event I've ever been involved in." When baseball star Cal Ripken waved the green flag that day to start the race, Jeff said, "That was the only flag that wasn't red, white, and blue."

Jeff clinched the points championship after the second-to-last race of the year, with a sixth-place finish at Atlanta in the NAPA 500.

Some drivers might have cruised through the final race of the year, but that was not Jeff's style. He tries to win each and every race he runs. So, with the championship already won, he drove for the lead.

Jeff was running out in front at the race in Loudon, New Hampshire, when Robby Gordon bumped him out of the lead in the closing stages and Jeff finished 15th.

". . . things just clicked."

Jeff won the Winston Cup championship for the fourth time in 2001, joining Richard Petty and Dale Earnhardt as the only drivers to win more than three. For Jeff, this championship was different from the others. It was the first for him as a car owner, and it was the first for most of his teammates. Fans had stopped yelling nasty things at Robbie Loomis.

With the championship won, Rick Hendrick said, "If you looked at this team at the end of 1999, the crew chief left, the pit crew left, the chief mechanic left. Robbie Loomis was man enough to take that challenge and come on board. I thought it would take longer than it has to build a championship team. But things just clicked."

Jeff raced in 37 races during the 2001 season. He started seven of them from the pole position and won six of them. He finished in the top 15 in 19 races and in the top 10 in 24 races. He earned $6,649,976 just from racing. Combining that figure with commercial endorsements, he earned more than $10 million.

In December 2001, Jeff was able to add another honor to his already impressive career. He carried the Olympic torch

Jeff carried the Olympic torch in Daytona Beach, Florida, in 2001. (Associated Press)

in Daytona, Florida. The torch was on its way to Salt Lake City, Utah, the site of the 2002 Winter Olympic Games.

End of the Marriage

The year 2002 was a tough one for Jeff both on and off the track. In addition to being a driver, he was a car owner. Jeff already had experience as being owner of his own team. But, in 2002, with Rick Hendrick, Jeff became the co-owner of rookie Jimmie Johnson's racing team. That added new responsibilities and new headaches to Jeff's already busy schedule.

But the biggest problems Jeff had in 2002 were personal. That was the year that he and Brooke separated. It was not a quiet separation. News of the marital split made huge headlines in just about all of the gossip papers.

Jeff remembered the frustration: "I was still racing," he said, "and Rick and I had a new team we were managing, but nobody wanted to talk about that. Every week I had to field questions about my personal life."

Now, in addition to his racing responsibilities, Jeff seemed to spend every spare moment with lawyers, taking care of all of the painful details that go along with a divorce.

Jeff may not have realized it, but he was suffering from exhaustion—both physical and emotional. It showed in his driving performances. He was leading the Daytona 500 when a miscue caused him to spin out.

In an incident that was clearly his own fault, Jeff spun out in the pits at Pocono, Pennsylvania. He crashed at Bristol, Tennessee, and then again at Martinsville, Virginia—both tracks where he usually did very well.

In the meantime, Jimmie Johnson, the rookie whose car Jeff co-owned, was doing very well. In fact he was doing better than any rookie had ever done before. In his first dozen Winston Cup races, Johnson had two wins and six top 10 finishes.

"It was a little embarrassing having the rookie driver whose car I co-owned winning two races before I'd sniffed a victory," Jeff recalled.

End of the Drought

Jeff's on-track drought ended in late August at Bristol. He qualified first and started on the pole. For much of the race, Jeff chased Rusty Wallace for the lead. Time and time again Jeff tried to pass but Rusty moved to block him. Finally, Jeff tapped the tail end of Rusty's car with his grille, just hard enough to make Rusty's car wiggle. That forced Rusty to step off the gas for a split second and Jeff used the opportunity to pass for the lead. Rusty was spitting mad but could not catch Jeff, whose winless streak was now over.

Jeff proved the Bristol win was no fluke when he won at Darlington, South Carolina, on September 1 for his second consecutive victory.

After Darlington, Gordon had run in 318 Winston Cup races and he had won 60 of them. It was the fifth time Gordon had won the Southern 500, tying Cale Yarborough for the record. It was the sixth time overall that Gordon has finished first at the 1.366-mile Darlington track.

The final restart of the race came with 45 laps left to go, and it was at this point that Gordon made his move,

Ending an on-track drought, Jeff won the NASCAR Sharpie 500 in Bristol, Tennessee, on August 24, 2002. (Associated Press)

taking the lead for keeps. He finished 1.734 seconds ahead of second-place Ryan Newman.

Gordon said, "In traffic I was awful—real tight. But on new tires I was unreal—I could really smoke around the bottom. We had a good car all day and once they [the pit crew] busted off a great stop and got me into third, the car was just awesome—it was 'Adios.' I just blew by those guys and I said, 'Boy, I've got to keep this thing out in the clean air [away from traffic].' My guys kept me out in clean air after that and made great adjustments on the car—what an incredible day."

Running Slow at Richmond

Jeff's hot streak cooled in Richmond the following weekend on Saturday night, September 7, 2002. He also blew a chance to gain ground on Sterling Marlin and Jeff Burton who were ahead of him in the points standings. Burton spun into turn three's outside wall early in the race. Soon thereafter, points leader Marlin and Jimmy Spencer also crashed. Marlin was done for the day, his first "did not finish" of the year.

Jeff had a golden opportunity to gain ground in the points race, but that is not how it turned out. Gordon had engine problems during the race, and spent too much time in the garage. When he came back out he stayed in the slow groove and simply got some laps in.

It was not Gordon's weekend. Sure, he lost his chance to win three Winston Cup races consecutively, but his sour luck started long before that. His problems began way back during the week's preliminary festivities when, during a golf cart race involving Looney Tunes characters, Jeff fell out of his golf cart. Luckily he was not injured. His bad luck became more serious later in the week when he crashed the car he had qualified in and had to start the Richmond race from the back of the pack in a backup car.

Jeff had another dismal performance at the Martinsville Speedway on October 20, 2002. He finished 36th; his chances of winning the championship were just about shredded.

Gordon said, "It's disappointing. We want to be a factor for the championship. We know that every race is critical.

We're not even going to talk about points for the rest of the season, we're just going to go out there and do everything we can to win races. We had that [lug nut] problem in the pits and came back from that, which was great. We got our track position back and just had a super car. I got on the outside, my car wasn't very good on the outside, and some guys got by me on the inside. I was just waiting to get back down and [Jeff] Burton came off the corner—I don't know if he got loose or what—he just turned sideways and turned right into me, put me in the wall, and from then on our day was pretty much done. We were three laps down and just riding around out there."

At the end of the 2002, Tony Stewart was the new Winston Cup champ. Jeff was fourth in the standings.

Show Business

NASCAR took another big step into the mainstream on January 11, 2003, when Jeff Gordon hosted the popular NBC TV show *Saturday Night Live*. According to sports consultant Neal Pilson, "There was a period of time when people didn't think of NASCAR stars in the same breath as an NBA star or a baseball star—and now they are beginning to do that."

Before the show, Jeff sounded a little uncertain about what he had gotten himself into. "I'm scared to death in a lot of ways," he said. "But each day [of rehearsal] that goes by, you become more and more comfortable. This is certainly nothing I'm used to doing."

Gordon agreed to appear on the show under a couple conditions: None of the comedy was to be detrimental to the sport of stock car racing, and there would be no references to Jeff's recent personal problems.

"I don't want to limit the writers and what they can come up with creatively, but I told them there were some areas to stay away from. Some of the things will be embarrassing," Gordon said again, before the show. "Nothing's going to take away from the sport."

When the show was over and all of the skits had gone smoothly, Jeff told a reporter that the adrenaline flow he felt while being on the stage was "like nothing I've ever experienced in my life. On the other shows you're doing interviews about things you know about. And it only lasts a couple of minutes. On *Saturday Night Live* they put you in skits and actually asked me to act. They do all the work, but it's up to you to be funny. The chance to bomb is just overwhelming."

The gig on *Saturday Night Live* was not Jeff's only journey into the world of showbiz. He has made several appearances on *The Late Show with David Letterman* and *The Tonight Show with Jay Leno*. He has also been a substitute

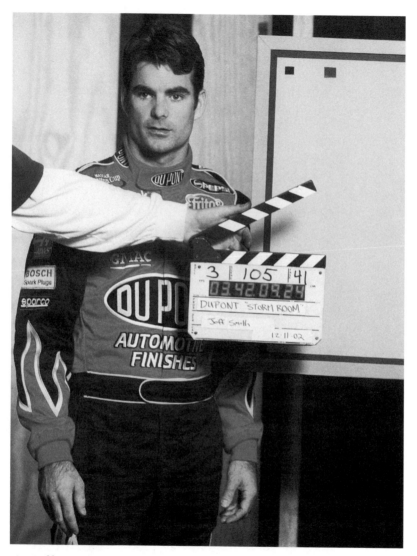

As Jeff's career and the popularity of NASCAR spread, he was in demand for many TV appearances and commercial endorsements. (Associated Press)

cohost a couple of times on the *Live with Regis and Kelly* morning talk show.

About substituting for Regis Philbin, Jeff says, "I have a great time. I always meet interesting people, and it's good exposure for our sport and our sponsors. If I could say yes every time they call, I certainly would. But my commitments are such that I can't."

Fourth Place . . . Again

Jeff was a contender to win the Winston Cup championship for the first half of the 2003 season. But in mid-season his hopes for another championship were dashed. Then there were four straight races in which Jeff did not finish. At the beginning of October, Jeff had only one win for the year. But that changed when he took the checkered flag two straight weeks at Martinsville and Atlanta.

Matt Kenseth was the 2003 Winston Cup champ. Hendrick Motorsports had three cars in the top 10 in the Winston Cup points standings. Jeff finished fourth for the second year in a row. His teammate Jimmie Johnson finished second, and Terry Labonte finished 10th.

In November 2003 Jeff sold the Florida home he had formerly shared with Brooke. He received $13 million for the house and another $2 million for the furnishings.

Jeff's Memoirs

Unlike many famous figures, Jeff decided not to wait until his golden years to share his experiences with his fans. During the off-season between the 2002 and 2003 racing seasons, even though he was only 31 years old, Jeff wrote his memoirs.

With the help of writer Steve Eubanks, Jeff wrote *Racing Back to the Front—My Memoir*, which was released during the 2003 season. The book probably should have been called *My Life—So Far*, because it is clear that Jeff's story is one that is far from over.

Jeff autographs a copy of his memoir for an excited fan. (Landov)

New Sponsor, New Rules

NASCAR made a couple of changes for the 2004 season. For one thing, Winston Cigarettes was no longer a primary sponsor, so the points championship was now called the Nextel Cup, after its new sponsor, a wireless communications company.

The other change involved the awarding of points. For the first time since 1975, there was a major adjustment in how the points champion would be determined.

From now on the last 10 races of the season would be a "Chase for the Championship." After 26 races in the 36-race season only drivers who are in the top 10 in points, or who are within 400 points of the lead, are eligible to win points.

"The Chase for the Championship will provide a better opportunity for more drivers to win the championship, creating excitement and drama throughout the entire season," NASCAR president Mike Helton said. "In addition, the Chase for the Championship will showcase our drivers' talents, increasing the value for all teams and their sponsors."

Since no driver who was not in the top 10 after 26 races has ever come back to win the championship, the changes should not limit the number of possible winners.

But a driver who finishes in the top 10 will have a better chance of winning than he did in previous years. That is because large leads will be wiped out. The first-place driver will be given a small five-point lead over the second-place driver, a 10-point lead over the third-place driver, a 15-point lead over the fourth-place driver, and so on.

The changes were made in reaction to Matt Kenseth's championship season in 2003. Kenseth built up a huge lead during the first two-thirds of the season, and then cruised the rest of the way, taking no chances, and he still won the championship easily. As of 2004 that would no longer be possible. Once the "Chase" began, his large lead would have been wiped out. There would be no "cruising."

About the changes Gordon said, "For the first 26 races, you're going to race basically like you did before. It's going to be important to be in that top 10. After race 26, it's totally different. That's exactly what they wanted to do. It's going to come down to being aggressive, being smart, and being lucky. That's going to make things exciting.

"I like the tracks in the last 10 races. They're good tracks for us. Our chances are good. We've got to make sure we're in that top 10. Then I think we'd have a great shot at winning more championships."

Although all of the teams will run in all of the races, critics of the new system say that those who do not finish in the top 10 will have less reason to run hard than they had before.

"We had some spectacular years . . ."

At the start of the 2004 season Jeff was asked if he worried about not winning as many races as he once had. He replied,

> Not really. I recognize that we had some very spectacular years and those weren't normal years when we were winning 10 or more races a year, year after year. I recognize how special that was then and how what I'm doing now is really more normal. My focus has turned so much more on winning the championship now. The way the point system has been in the past, winning a lot of races doesn't necessarily win you the championship. This year, the focus is going to be more on winning—especially during the last 10 races. I think you're going to see us racing a little bit different. You'll see guys making bigger decisions and taking more chances. Of course, the tires and the downforce on the cars is going to change as well. But it doesn't bother me. I've had enough success in this sport and I've enjoyed a lot of great things—championships and wins—that if I don't win 10 races, it doesn't bother me.

The Future

Jeff's charity work continues. In 2001 the Jeff Gordon Foundation teamed up with the children's show *Sesame*

Jeff Gordon has become a role model and inspiration, both on and off the track. (Landov)

Street, and in 2004 helped celebrate that show's 35th anniversary. To make money for children's charities, the Foundation sells die-cast models of Jeff's car with Sesame Street characters, such as Elmo and Cookie Monster, painted on them.

Jeff does not plan to stay a race car driver forever. On the other hand, he does not think he will ever be able to turn his back on stock car racing completely. Chances are he will become a full-time team owner like Rick Hendrick and continue in the business with some other "kid" doing the job behind the steering wheel.

Jeff believes he has become more relaxed as he has matured. "I'm very comfortable with who I am right now and what my role is and what I have to do on and off the track."

TIME LINE

1971   Born August 4 in Vallejo, California

1979   Wins quarter midget national championship at age eight

1981   Wins quarter midget national championship for the second time

1989   Named USAC midget Rookie of the Year

1990   Wins USAAC National Midget Championship at age 19, the youngest driver ever to do so

1991   Named Busch series Rookie of the Year

1992   Leads Busch series drivers in money earned; drives in first Winston Cup race, at the Atlanta Motor Speedway; his first Winston Cup race is also "King" Richard Petty's last race

1993   Named the Winston Cup Rookie of the Year

1994 Wins the inaugural Brickyard 400, the first stock car race ever held at the Indianapolis Motor Speedway; marries former Miss Winston, Brooke Sealey, in Charlotte, North Carolina

1995 Becomes the youngest driver of the modern era to win the Winston Cup championship

1996 Wins 10 Winston Cup races but finishes second to Terry Labonte for the championship

1997 Wins the Winston Cup championship for the second time; wins the Daytona 500, the youngest driver ever to do so

1998 Wins the Winston Cup championship for the third time, scoring 13 victories in the process; wins the Brickyard 400 for the second time

1999 Wins seven Winston Cup races, the fifth straight year he has finished first among drivers in Winston Cup victories; establishes the Jeff Gordon Foundation, a charity organization for children's causes

2000 Wins his 50th Winston Cup race

2001 Wins the Winston Cup championship for the fourth time; becomes first stock car driver to earn more than $10 million in a single year

2002 Becomes co-owner of a racing team; wins 60th Winston Cup race and surpasses the $50 million mark in career earnings; separates from Brooke; finishes fourth in points standings

2003 Makes many TV appearances, including guest host slot on *Saturday Night Live;* finishes in fourth place again

HOW TO BECOME A PROFESSIONAL ATHLETE

THE JOB

Professional athletes can participate in team sports such as baseball, basketball, and football, or in individual sports such as cycling, tennis, figure skating, golf, running, or boxing. Professional athletes compete against other athletes or teams to win prizes and money. Here we will focus mainly on becoming a professional athlete in an individual sport.

Depending on the nature of the specific sport, most athletes compete against a field of individuals. The field of competitors can be as small as one (tennis, boxing) or as large as the number of qualified competitors, anywhere from six to 30 (figure skating, cycling, race car driving). In certain individual events, such as the marathon or triathlon, the field may seem excessively large—often tens of thousands of runners compete in the New York City Marathon—but for the professional runners competing in the race, only a handful of other runners represent real competition.

The athletic performances of those in individual sports are evaluated according to the nature and rules of each specific sport. For example, the winner of a footrace is whoever crosses the finish line first; in tennis the winner is the one who scores the highest in a set number of games; in boxing and figure skating the winners are determined by a panel of judges. Competitions are organized by local, regional, national, and international organizations and associations whose primary functions are to promote the sport and sponsor competitive events. Within a professional sport there are usually different levels of competition based on age, ability, and gender. There are often different designations and events within one sport. Tennis, for example, consists of doubles and singles, while track and field contains many different events, from field events such as the javelin and shot put, to track events such as the 110-meter dash and the two-mile relay race.

Athletes train year-round, on their own or with a coach, friend, parent, or trainer. In addition to stretching and exercising the specific muscles used in any given sport, athletes concentrate on developing excellent eating and sleeping habits that will help them remain in top condition throughout the year. Although certain sports have a particular season, most professional athletes train rigorously all year, varying the type and duration of their workouts to develop strength, cardiovascular ability, flexibility, endurance, speed, and quickness, as well as to focus on technique and control. Often an athlete's training focuses less on the overall game or program that the athlete will execute than on specific areas or details of that game or program. Figure skaters, for example, won't simply keep going through their entire long programs from start to finish but instead will focus on the jumps, turns, and hand movements that refine the program. Similarly, sprinters don't run only the sprint distances they race in during a meet; instead, they vary their workouts to include some distance work, some sprints, a lot of weight training to build strength, and maybe some mental exercises to build control and focus while in the starter's blocks. Tennis players routinely spend hours just practicing their forehand, down-the-line shots.

Athletes often watch videotapes or films of their previous practices or competitions to see where they can improve their performance. They also study what the other competitors are doing in order to prepare strategies for winning.

REQUIREMENTS
High School

A high school diploma will provide you with the basic skills you will need in your long climb to becoming a professional athlete. Business and mathematics classes will teach you how to manage money wisely. Speech classes will help you become a better communicator. Physical education classes will help you build your strength, agility, and competitive spirit. You should, of course, participate in every organized sport that your school offers and that interests you.

Some individual sports such as tennis and gymnastics have professional competitors who are high school students. Teenagers in this situation often have private coaches with whom they practice both before and after going to school, and others are homeschooled as they travel to competitions.

Postsecondary Training

There are no formal education requirements for sports, although certain competitions and training opportunities are only available to those enrolled in four-year colleges and universities. Collegiate-level competitions are where most athletes in this area hone their skills; they may also compete in international or national competitions outside of college, but the chance to train and receive an education isn't one many serious athletes refuse. In fact, outstanding ability in athletics is the way many students pay for their college educations. Given the chances of striking it rich financially, an education (especially a free one) is a wise investment and one fully supported by most professional sports organizations.

Other Requirements

There is so much competition to be among the world's elite athletes in any given sport that talent alone isn't the primary requirement. Diligence, perseverance, hard work, ambition, and courage are all essential qualities to the individual who dreams of making a career as a professional athlete. "If you want to be a pro, there's no halfway. There's no three-quarters way," says Eric Roller, a former professional tennis player who competed primarily on the Florida circuit. Other specific requirements will vary according to the sport. Jockeys, for example, are usually petite men and women.

EXPLORING

If you are interested in pursuing a career in professional sports you should start participating in that sport as much and as early as possible. With some sports, an individual who is 15 may already be too old to realistically begin pursuing a professional career. By playing the sport and by talking to coaches, trainers, and athletes in the field, you can ascertain whether you like the sport enough to make it a career, determine if you have enough talent, and gain new insight into the field. You can also contact professional organizations and associations for information on how to best prepare for a career in their sport. Sometimes there are specialized training programs available, and the best way to find out is to get in contact with the people whose job it is to promote the sport.

EMPLOYERS

Professional athletes who compete in individual sports are not employed in the same manner as most workers. They do not work for employers, but choose the competitions or tournaments they wish to compete in. For example, a professional runner may choose to enter the Boston Marathon and then travel to Atlanta for the Peachtree Road Race.

STARTING OUT

Professional athletes must meet the requirements established by the organizing bodies of their respective sport.

Sometimes this means meeting a physical requirement such as age, height, or weight; sometimes it means fulfilling a number of required stunts, or participating in a certain number of competitions. Professional organizations usually arrange it so that athletes can build up their skills and level of play by participating in lower-level competitions. College sports, as mentioned above, are an excellent way to improve one's skills while pursuing an education.

ADVANCEMENT

Professional athletes advance into the elite numbers of their sport by working and practicing hard, and by winning. Professional athletes usually obtain representation by sports agents in the behind-the-scenes deals that determine for which teams they will be playing and what they will be paid. These agents also may be involved with other key decisions involving commercial endorsements, personal income taxes, and financial investments of the athlete's revenues.

A college education can prepare all athletes for the day when their bodies can no longer compete at the top level, whether because of age or an unforeseen injury. Every athlete should be prepared to move into another career, related to the world of sports or not.

EARNINGS

The U.S. Department of Labor reports that athletes had median annual earnings of $45,320 in 2002. The lowest paid 10 percent earned less than $14,090, and the highest paid 10 percent made more than $145,600, with the top athletes making considerably more.

Salaries, prize monies, and commercial endorsements will vary from sport to sport; a lot depends on the popularity of the sport and its ability to attract spectators, or on the sport's professional organization and its ability to drum up sponsors for competitions and prize money. Still other sports, like boxing, depend on the skill of the fight's promoters to create interest in the fight. An elite professional tennis player who wins Wimbledon, for example, usually earns over half a million dollars in a matter of several hours. Add to that the incredible sums a Wimbledon champion can make in endorsements and the tennis star can earn over $1 million a year. This scenario is misleading, however; to begin with, top athletes usually cannot perform at such a level for very long, which is why a good accountant and investment counselor comes in handy. Secondly, for every top athlete who earns millions of dollars in a year, there are hundreds of professional athletes who earn less than $40,000. The stakes are incredibly high, the competition fierce.

Perhaps the only caveat to the financial success of an elite athlete is the individual's character or personality. An athlete with a bad temper or prone to unsportsmanlike behavior may still be able to set records or win games, but he or she won't necessarily be able to cash in on commercial endorsements. Advertisers are notoriously fickle about the spokespeople they choose to endorse products; some athletes have lost million-dollar accounts because of their bad behavior on and off the field of play.

Other options exist for the professional athlete who has reached the end of his or her career. Many go into some area of coaching, sports administration, management, or broadcasting. The professional athlete's unique insight and perspective can be a real asset in careers in these areas. Other athletes have been simultaneously pursuing other interests, some completely unrelated to their sport, such as education, business, social welfare, or the arts. Many continue to stay involved with the sport they have loved since childhood, coaching young children or volunteering with local school teams.

WORK ENVIRONMENT

Athletes compete in many different conditions, according to the setting of the sport (indoors or outdoors) and the rules of the organizing or governing bodies. Track-and-field athletes often compete in hot or rainy conditions, but at any point organizing officials can call off the meet or postpone competition until better weather. Indoor events are less subject to cancellation. However, since it is in the best interests of an organization not to risk the athletes' health, any condition that might adversely affect the outcome of a competition is usually reason enough to cancel or postpone it. An athlete, on the other hand, may withdraw from competition if he or she is injured or ill. Nerves and fear are not good reasons to default on a competition, and part of ascending into the ranks of professional athletes means learning to cope with the anxiety that competition brings. Some athletes actually thrive on the nervous tension.

In order to reach the elite level of any sport, athletes must begin their careers early. Most professional athletes have been working at their sports since they were small children; skiers, figure skaters, and gymnasts, for example, begin skiing, skating, and tumbling as young as age two or three. Athletes have to fit hours of practice time into an already full day, usually several hours before school, and several hours after school. To make the situation more difficult, competitions and facilities for practice are often far from the young athlete's home, which means they either commute to and from practice and competitions with a parent, or they live with a coach or trainer for most of the year. Separation from a child's parents and family is an especially hard and frustrating element of the training program. When a child has demonstrated uncommon excellence in a sport, the family often decides to move to the city in which the sports facility is located, so that the child doesn't have to travel or be separated from a normal family environment.

The expenses of a sport can be overwhelming, as can the time an athlete must devote to practice and travel to and from competitions. In addition to specialized equipment and clothing, the athlete must pay for a coach, travel expenses, competition fees, and, depending on the sport, time at the facility or gym where he or she practices. Tennis, golf, figure skating, and skiing are among the most expensive sports to enter.

Even with the years of hard work, practice, and financial sacrifice that most athletes and their families must endure, there is no guarantee that an athlete will achieve the rarest of the rare in the sports world—financial reward. An athlete needs to truly love the sport at which he or she excels, and also have a nearly insatiable ambition and work ethic.

OUTLOOK

Again, the outlook will vary depending on the sport, its popularity, and the number of professional athletes currently competing. On the whole, the outlook for the field of professional sports is healthy, but the number of jobs will not increase dramatically. Some sports, however, may experience a rise in popularity, which will translate into greater opportunities for higher salaries, prize monies, and commercial endorsements.

TO LEARN MORE ABOUT PROFESSIONAL ATHLETES

BOOKS

Boyle, Michael. *Functional Training for Sports*. Champaign, Illinois: Human Kinetics, 2003.

Drury, Jennifer. *The Athlete's Guide to Sponsorship*. Boulder, Colo.: Velo Press, 2000.

Miller, G. Wayne. *Men and Speed: A Wild Ride through NASCAR's Breakout Season*. New York: PublicAffairs, 2002.

Martin, Mark. *NASCAR For Dummies*. Hoboken, N.J.: Wiley, 2000.

Menzer, Joe. *The Wildest Ride: A History of NASCAR*. New York: Simon & Schuster, 2002.

NASCAR. *Official NASCAR Trivia: The Ultimate Challenge for NASCAR Fans.* New York: HarperEntertainment, 1998.

WEBSITES AND ORGANIZATIONS

Young people who are interested in becoming professional athletes should contact the professional organizations for the sport in which they would like to compete, such as the National Hockey League, NASCAR, the U.S. Tennis Association, the Professional Golfer's Association, or the National Bowling Association. Ask for information on requirements, training centers, coaches, and so on.

For a free brochure and information on the Junior Olympics and more, write to
Amateur Athletic Union
c/o The Walt Disney World Resort
P.O. Box 10000
Lake Buena Vista, FL 32830-1000
http://www.aausports.org

For additional information on athletics, contact
American Alliance for Health, Physical Education, Recreation, and Dance
1900 Association Drive
Reston, VA 20191
http://www.aahperd.org

The popular magazine *Sports Illustrated for Kids* also has a website.

Sports Illustrated for Kids

http://www.sikids.com

Visit the U.S. Olympic Committee's website for the latest sporting news and information about upcoming Olympic competitions.

United States Olympic Committee

http://www.olympic-usa.org

The following website provides information about and links to women in all kinds of sports:

Women in Sports

http://www.makeithappen.com/wis/index.html

TO LEARN MORE ABOUT JEFF GORDON AND STOCK CAR RACING

BOOKS

Benson, Michael, ed. *Stock Car Spectacular*. New York: Crescent Books, 1995.

Benson, Michael. *Women in Racing*. Philadelphia: Chelsea House Publishers, 1997.

Garfield, Ken. *Jeff Gordon: Rewriting the Record Book*. Charlotte, N.C.: Sports Publishing L.L.C., 2001.

Gordon, Jeff, and Steve Eubanks. *Jeff Gordon: Racing Back to the Front—My Memoir*. New York: Atria Books, 2003.

Martin, Ronda Jackson. *Stock Car Legends*. Nashville, Tenn.: Premium Press America, 1994.

Stewart, Mark. *Jeff Gordon: Rainbow Warrior*. Brookfield, Conn.: The Millbrook Press Inc., 2000.

MAGAZINES AND NEWSPAPERS

"Driven to Sell." *New York Post*, November 22, 2003, p. 8R.

Tuschak, Beth. "Jeff Gordon: Manhattan Man about Town." (New York) *Daily News*, November 30, 2003, Special Section, p. 3.

WEBSITES AND ORGANIZATIONS

Want to see Jeff race? Start here for info regarding schedules, tickets, hotels, and NASCAR team apparel and collectibles.

Jeff Gordon Online

http://www.jeffgordononline.com

The following is the official website of the National Association of Stock Car Automobile Racing:

NASCAR.COM

http://www.nascar.com

The following museum is open 9:00 A.M. to 5:00 P.M. daily. Admission: $5 adults; kids under 12 free.

Darlington Raceway Stock Car Museum

1301 Harry Byrd Highway

P.O. Box 500

Darlington, SC 29532

http://www.darlingtonraceway.com

The following museum is open 8:00 A.M. to 5:00 P.M. daily, except Thanksgiving, Christmas, and Easter.

The International Motorsports Hall of Fame and Museum

P.O. Box 1018

Talladega, AL 35161

Tel: (256) 362-5002

http://www.motorsportshalloffame.com

STOCK CAR RACING GLOSSARY

apron paved portion of a racetrack that separates the racing surface itself from the (usually unpaved) infield

banking the sloping of a racetrack, particularly at the curve or corner, from the apron to the outside wall; the degree of banking is determined by measuring that slope against the horizon

checkered flag waved to signal the winner of the race

chute racetrack straightaway

downforce the pressure of the air on a car as it races; downforce increases with velocity—that is, the faster a car is going, the greater the downforce upon it; the correct amount of downforce is necessary for the car to handle properly

drafting practice of two or more cars running nose-to-tail while racing, almost touching, like a train: the lead car, by displacing the air around it, creates a vacuum between its rear end and the nose of the car behind it; because of this the second car is actually pulled along by the first car; cars in a long line can form a drafting train in which every car, except for the car in the front, is getting a tow

green flag waved to signal the start of a race, or a restart if it follows a caution period

groove best route around a racetrack; the most efficient and/or quickest route around the track for a particular driver; the *high groove* takes a car closer to the outside wall for most of a lap; the *low groove* takes a car closer to the apron than the outside wall

handling generally, a car's performance when racing, qualifying or practicing; how a car handles is determined by its tires, suspension geometry, aerodynamics, and other factors

loose handling condition describing the tendency of a car's rear wheels to break away from the pavement, swinging its rear end toward the outside wall (fishtailing); also called *oversteer*

NASCAR National Association of Stock Car Automobile Racing

pit road road that leads from the racing surface to the pit area

pits   area of a racetrack, off the racing surface, where a car stops for servicing

push   handling characteristic of a car during which its front end tends to "push" or "plow" toward the outside wall in a corner; also known as *understeer*

short track   speedway that measures less than a mile around

superspeedway   largest and fastest racetracks

tri-oval   racetrack that has a *hump* or *fifth turn* in addition to the standard four corners; not to be confused with a triangle-shaped speedway, which has only three distinct turns

USAC   United States Automobile Club

white flag   waved to signal one lap left in the race

yellow flag   waved to signal caution, or a problem on the track; cars must slow down and passing is forbidden

INDEX

Page numbers in *italics* indicate illustrations.

ABOUT THE AUTHOR

Michael Benson is the former editor of *Stock Car Spectacular* magazine. He has written biographies for children about Dale Earnhardt Sr., Ronald Reagan, Bill Clinton, William Howard Taft, Malcolm X, Muhammad Ali, Hank Aaron, Lance Armstrong, Wayne Gretzky, and Gloria Estefan. He also edited *All-Time Baseball Greats*, and *Fight Game* magazines and is the author of more than 30 books, including *The Encyclopedia of the JFK Assassination* and *Complete Idiot's Guides to NASA, The CIA, National Security, Aircraft Carriers, Submarines,* and *Modern China.* Originally from Rochester, New York, he is a graduate of Hofstra University. He enjoys his life with his wife and two children in Brooklyn, New York. His goal is to one day write the Great American Novel.

The author wishes to acknowledge the following persons and organizations without whose help the creation of this book would have been impossible: Barry C. Altmark, James Chambers, Jake Elwell, Norman Jacobs, NASCAR, and the whole staff of *Stock Car Spectacular* magazine. He dedicates this book to Paul Johnson.